STATEN ISLAND

1524 · 1898

Staten Island
1524 ⁄ 1898

By HENRY G. STEINMEYER

Revised edition

Published by

THE STATEN ISLAND HISTORICAL SOCIETY

RICHMONDTOWN, STATEN ISLAND, N. Y.

1987

Frontispiece: *"The Narrows from the Pavilion near the Quarantine Ground Staten Island."* Drawn by E. W. Clay and engraved by R. Hirshelwood, New York, 1835. Staten Island Historical Society (SIHS).

The Staten Island Historical Society is an independent non-profit cultural organization that manages Richmondtown Restoration for the city of New York. The city of New York owns the land and buildings of Richmondtown Restoration and supports part of its operations with public funds provided by the Department of Cultural Affairs. Richmondtown Restoration also receives support from the New York State Department of Education, the New York State Council on the Arts, corporations, foundations, and private individuals.

First published in 1950 by the Staten Island Historical Society.
Revised edition © 1987 Staten Island Historical Society.
Published with the assistance of the John Frederick Smith Publication Fund.

Library of Congress Cataloging-in-Publication Data

Steinmeyer, Henry G., 1886–1980.
Staten Island, 1524–1898.

Bibliography: p. 105.
Includes index.
1. Staten Island (New York, N.Y.) — History.
2. New York (N.Y.) — History.
3. Staten Island (New York, N.Y.) — Description — Views.
4. New York (N.Y.) — Description — Views. I. Title.
F127.S7S78 1987   974.7´26   87-6525
ISBN 0-89062-223-X

Cover design by Romeo Enriquez.

Cover: *The Narrows "between Red and Yellow Hook, on Long Island, & the East Bluff of Staten Island,"* 1777. Staten Island Institute of Arts and Sciences.

CONTENTS

Voorlezer's House, Richmondtown Restoration, built ca. 1696; restored 1942 and 1985. Photograph by William McMillen, 1986. SIHS.

FOREWORD TO NEW EDITION

SINCE its first publication in 1950 this small volume has served as an invaluable introduction to our island's early history. Henry G. Steinmeyer (1886-1980) was a member of the farsighted corps of volunteers who worked for the Staten Island Historical Society in the 1930s and 1940s and later established Richmondtown Restoration. A native of Staten Island, he lived for twenty-nine years at 74 Arthur Kill Road in Richmondtown, originally the home of the Dutch reformed minister and now known as the Parsonage. Aside from his practice of dentistry, he found time for a diversity of literary work and community service. He wrote and published poetry and short stories and organized and conducted his own orchestra. His love of horses found expression in the Bridle Path Association of Richmond County. His first historical publication, "An Island Childhood," in the April 1939 issue of the *Staten Island Historian,* was followed by other articles on the Revolutionary War era, theater and opera performances on Staten Island, private school buildings, and a South Beach resort. He served as editor of the *Staten Island Historian* from 1955 to 1969.

As the physical evidence of our historic landscape and built environment gives way to rapid growth, Dr. Steinmeyer's work stands out in greater relief and is here presented with renewed appreciation. In this edition, the original text is reproduced in facsimile, but many new illustrations have been added. Most of the original illustrations have been included, but they have now been inserted at appropriate points in the narrative, with dating retained from the first edition.

Barnett Shepherd, Executive Director
Staten Island Historical Society
January 1987

[7]

FOREWORD

STATEN ISLAND has never lacked able writers to record the stirring events which comprise its history. The first to write from an historic viewpoint was Reverend Peter I. Van Pelt, minister of the Reformed Dutch Church at Port Richmond, whose "Brief History of the Settlement of Staten Island" was published in 1818. There followed in chronological order Raymond M. Tysen, whose lectures on the history of the Island were published in 1842; Charles Edward Anthon, whose notes taken in 1850 were published in the "Proceedings of the Staten Island Institute of Arts and Sciences" during the years 1925-1932; and Gabriel P. Disosway who published many newspaper articles between 1859 and 1866.

The first attempt at a conclusive history of Staten Island was made in 1877, when John J. Clute published his "Annals of Staten Island". In 1887 Richard M. Bayles, a professional historian, contributed his "History of Richmond County", and in 1898-1900 Ira K. Morris brought out his "Memorial History of Staten Island".

The most exhaustive and complete history is "Staten Island and Its People", published in 1930 and written by the late Charles W. Leng and William T. Davis. Added to the works of these authors are the efforts of many writers which have appeared in the publications of the Staten Island Institute of Arts and Sciences and the Staten Island Historical Society. These form veritable mines of historical miscellany.

To the latter Society and to one of its members, Henry G. Steinmeyer, we are indebted for this present work. The Society was incorporated in 1856 to "preserve whatever relates to the history of Staten Island", and has since come to occupy a respected position, not only in its community, but in the roster of similar societies throughout the country. Its well-balanced program of local history appreciation and its splendid museum, both administered by volunteers, are responsible for this position. Dr. Steinmeyer's work is a further step in this program and his study of our history and frequent contributions to its writings qualify him for the work he has undertaken.

This book is the result of a widespread desire for a concise, popularly written history adapted to the means and the reading time of everyone. The former histories are available only at libraries and will always be the main sources of historical research.

Staten Island stands at the crossroads of an important period in her history. Vast so-called "public improvements" such as arterial parkways, public housing, widened highways and land fill projects, threaten as never before to engulf and destroy the last material vestiges of our history. The Staten Island Historical Society believes that in presenting this book to the public it may serve to help stimulate an interest in our Island and in the preservation of its landmarks.

LORING McMILLEN,
Borough Historian

Bescrevinge van 't Eijlant de Zuidhoek de Engenwsten tijdt van de gevaren bij Eijbeck Wuhostinckel de Langh Eijlant. Cruijdt bij weder york
A' kde comunt eijlant B Ce gadt om in te houd B C de spanhound D Koud eilant c cerck E schijs hound die did nad der hnid om na houde houleijhen wolken dijdt
banket door dan gerhend te SSory van bijen D E F de lant gerwinck de westinckel F de kil van kot. die allet ter ere bije van elangt eijlant te haent
ver jagde hurt op nafag.

I

The Adventurers

MANY SUNS had risen since the great ship's departure, and the savages, grown weary of watching for its return, finally ceased scanning the eastern horizon and went away to resume their fishing. The craft, so immense to their eyes, was in their thoughts all through that year; amongst themselves they talked of it while weaving seines, and while they fashioned arrows and restrung the bows which sped flint-tipped missiles on long, lethal flights.

The ship which in 1524 had anchored for so brief a period was the *Dolphin,* commanded by an Italian in the employ of Francis I of France. His name was Giovanni da Verrazzano, and he, along with his royal patron and many other navigators and influential individuals, was obsessed with the notion that a short cut to the East Indies and their glittering riches could be found by sailing west. He cruised the eastern coast of North America from the Carolinas to Nova Scotia, put ashore at various points, and set down in his report all he was able to learn concerning the natives and the country itself. There is no definite proof that in 1525 Estevan Gomez, searching for the identical passage, was a visitor to the vicinity of New York Bay, but he did sail the coast and left a chart to prove it. However, for more than seventy-five years—three quarters of a century—Europeans paid little attention to North America. If the Staten Island aborigines detected an occasional sail in the distance it must have been catching the breeze for the propulsion of some fisherman's or adventurer's vessel bound north or south.

The soil of the Island was fertile, and its diversified topography offered terrain which produced in abundance the variety of

View of the entrance of New York harbor from Najak [Fort Hamilton] by Jasper Danckaerts from Journal of a Voyage to New York and a Tour in Several of the American Colonies in 1679-1680, *by Jasper Danckaerts and Peter Sluyter. Brooklyn Historical Society.*

vegetation which supported the Indians who dwelt upon its shores and the wild animals which lived in its upland forests. The natives hunted deer and wild turkey, utilizing their flesh for food; they clothed themselves in the skins of wolves and wildcats. Oysters, as well as shad and other fish, were plentiful. There must have been bears on the Island during the early years, for we read that in the 17th century Governor Thomas Dongan was "engaged at his hunting lodge on Staten Island killing bears." In 1681 there was a bounty on wolves, and some were trapped in Jones' Wolf Pit, near Bull's Head. Remains of red foxes, as well as the bones of beaver, have been found in Indian fire-pits. Opossum, raccoon, and muskrat were common.

The Indians who lived upon the Island at the time when the first white men visited these shores were Algonkins, a branch of the indigenous population of the eastern part of North America, and these, divided into some thirty or more nations, were distributed throughout eastern Canada, the New England area, southern New York, Delaware and Pennsylvania. One of these was the Delaware nation, and two of its three divisions were Munceys and Unamis. Of the latter there were upon the Island members of three tribes: Tappans, Hackensacks, and Raritans. It is thought that not more than one hundred of these natives dwelt here, the others of their tribes being spread over a bit more territory than that which now comprises the Metropolitan area. Their culture was inferior to that of the other great eastern Indian nation, the Iroquois, but, like these, they dressed in skins and feathers and painted their faces. Their dome-shaped habitations were constructed of boughs tied together at the top and thatched with salt hay and were approximately thirty feet in circumference, with one entrance. A hole at the top served as outlet for the smoke of the fire which provided warmth, and over which food was prepared.

The Indians who had watched the *Dolphin* sail away over the far edge of their universe grew old, and when they died were interred, their bodies laid upon their sides, arms and legs flexed so that hands and feet were together close to the chin. Their children were in all likelihood dead. During the eighty-five years which had elapsed since Verrazzano's visit they had lived an almost wholly peaceful life, not given to that indulgence in constant warfare which seemed to occupy so much of the time of their inland neighbors, the Iroquois. But the year 1609 marked the termination of this Arcadian existence, for on September 3 of that year the redskins who at dawn looked out over the Narrows saw afar off a vessel in appearance much like the one the sight of which had so startled and astonished their ancestors who had crouched upon the same grassy knoll.

Europeans still were looking for a short route to India and Cathay, and the middle-aged navigator who stood upon the deck of the anchored ship was an Englishman named Henry Hudson, engaged by the Netherlands East India Company to search out the northwest passage. His boat was a two masted square rigged Dutch galiot of eighty tons burden called the *Half Moon,* and manned by a Dutch and English crew of twenty. Anchoring off Sandy Hook he had next morning sent a party to take soundings farther into the lower bay. Upon finding five fathoms depth close to shore he ventured in towards the Narrows and again dropped anchor. Robert Juet, mate, relates in his journal that ". . . our [long] boat went on land with our net to fish, and caught ten great mullets, of a foot and a half apiece, and a ray as great as four men could haul into the ship. . . . This day the people of the country came aboard of us, seeming very glad of our coming, and brought green tobacco, and gave us of it for knives and beads. They go in deer skins, well dressed. They have yellow copper. They desire clothes, and are very civil. They have great store of maize or Indian wheat, wherof they make good bread. The country is full of great and tall oaks."

Two days later, after having entertained many curious Indians aboard the *Half Moon,* Hudson sent one John Coleman, along with four other mariners, to sound the Narrows and the waters beyond it. The party proceeded as far as Newark Bay with no untoward incident, but as they were returning to the ship some Indians in a canoe discharged a flight of arrows at the white men, resulting in the death of Coleman, who had "an arrow shot into his throat." Immediately following this sudden and unlooked for manifestation of hostility the savages paddled off towards the shore, while the sounding party in a panic made off in the direction of their ship. Darkness fell, and the frightened survivors did not reach the *Half Moon* until ten next morning. Indians continued to visit the ship for bartering, none seeming to possess any knowledge concerning the affray of the previous day. Hudson, distrustful, had them closely watched, and on September 11, a fair and hot day, he weighed anchor and sailed in through the Narrows. "The people of the country came aboard of us," writes Juet, "making show of love, and gave us tobacco and Indian wheat, and departed for that night; but we durst not trust them."

Hudson slowly drifted to a point off the tip of Manhattan Island, where he again anchored, as the wind was ahead. Here he had time for a long look at the area that is now so familiar to the thousands of Staten Islanders who daily commute to business, and familiar, too, to countless thousands who remember it as their first view of the New World. All that Henry Hudson saw were a few wigwams in a wilderness of greenery, and it is doubtful that he devoted any of his predictive dreaming to the narrow strip off his starboard bow, for straight ahead lay the broad mouth of a river which, for aught he knew, might be the long sought route to the jewels and the spices and the silks of the East.

On September 14 he began his trip up the river and reached a point not far below what is now the city of Albany. Convinced that Asia lay not at the end of the narrowing stream which stretched ahead he turned, and on the 4th of October a group of aboriginal Staten Islanders saw the *Half Moon* pass through the Narrows on its passage back to Europe.

The Netherlands East India Company listened politely to Hudson's recital concerning the manifold attractions of the region he had visited, but their minds were on the Orient. The commander exhibited the bales of furs which he had brought back, but they evinced scant interest. As a matter of fact, Holland was doing a good business in furs with Russia. Easy money was what the aristocratic directors were out after, and peltries did not seem to be the answer. But there were other more perspicacious if less patrician Hollanders, and these saw no reason why they should pay the Emperor of Russia good coin of the realm for furs when for a few beads and knick-knacks they could procure the same merchandise from the American natives. And when a ship which they dispatched to the "great river," as Hudson called it, returned with its cargo of furs they nodded, passed around the schnapps, and decided that here was a pretty good thing.

The Indians of Staten Island may have watched an occasional ship sail up the bay; they may even have indulged in barter when outgoing vessels anchored off the great spring later called the Watering Place (Tompkinsville) to take on fresh water. But they continued to enjoy a sequestered existence for another thirty years, since no attempt was made by the

Dutch to settle in an area which was separated from the main-land by only a narrow stream. Even though the redskins of the Island were a peaceful lot, it did not follow that all their relatives to the westward were of like disposition. So the Hollanders did their fur trading far up the river and left the Staten Island Indians to their own devices. Our Raritans enjoyed the pleasant springs and summers, hunted wild creatures during the autumn, and huddled close together around their fires all winter. They had plenty of fish, flesh, suppaen, and succotash. And when they desired something especially tasty they boiled a couple of dogs. If they hankered after further contact with the fabulous beings who seemed so generous with their bright-colored beads and baubles it was only because they didn't know when they were well off.

View of New Amsterdam by Joost Hartgers, 1626-28. Shown in reverse of original printing. New-York Historical Society.

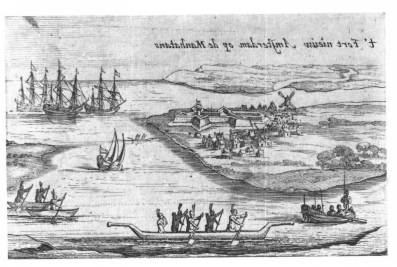

II

The First Settlements

A NEW ORGANIZATION, the Dutch West India
Company, was chartered in 1621. Its aims were pri-
marily commercial, but its articles provided for colonization,
and the first shipload of settlers brought over in the *New
Netherland* were taken to the head of the Hudson River, and
the fort subsequently erected there was called Fort Orange
(Albany). By 1625 the West India Company, aware that
the New Netherlands project was yielding substantial profits,
began to contemplate the establishment of a town on Manhattan Island, and presently had signed up forty-five individuals
who, with one hundred and three head of cattle and household
equipment, set sail. It was manifest that there had to be someone officially at the head of the colony, but since the Dutch
government refused to assume responsibility for the administration of its affairs the individual chosen was the selection of the
West India Company and held the title of director-general.
He was Peter Minuit, a man of middle age who had travelled
widely, and he arrived at Manhattan the 4th of July, 1626.
He took a hasty look about the place and two days later bought
the island from the Indians for twenty-four dollars worth of
flashy merchandize. By the time a few weeks had elapsed the
settlers had erected a rude blockhouse as well as a group of
dwellings, and were extending the hand of welcome to a fresh
consignment of immigrants. The population of Manhattan
was now two hundred souls. Staten Island was still un-
colonized and at the time bore more resemblance to the Garden
of Eden than at any period thereafter.

The patroon system next came into being. This was privi-
lege with a capital P, and if Minuit was astute enough to snap

up for twenty-four dollars land which he estimated to be twenty-two thousand acres in extent, there were other Dutchmen through whose arteries coursed the same type of blood. Among these was one Michael Pauw. In 1630 he picked out a tract of land which included not only all of Staten Island, but a great section of the Jersey shore, and his colony bore the name of Pavonia, or the Commune of Pauw (Communipaw). The other patroons did even better for themselves, and when the remaining members of the West India Company awakened to the realization that the best plums had been picked they raised a ruckus. So, for the sake of peace, the three original patroons sold the disgruntled directors some of their holdings, and as a result of this transaction Staten Island passed into the ownership of Captain David Pietersen De Vries. In January 1639 he shipped a small group of settlers to the Island and this constituted the first attempt at colonization. Wilhelm Kieft was now director-general, having succeeded the second governor, Van Twiller. A year later De Vries leased the plantation to Thomas Smythe, who seems to have met his end at the hands of Indians in reprisal for the unjustified killing of several of their number by a punitive expedition from Manhattan.

Although De Vries considered himself the owner of Staten Island he gave up his idea of personally governing it and went off into the valley of the Hackensack River to found a colony. Subsequently he allowed Kieft to send Cornelius Melyn to the Island in order to erect a distillery and to engage in the processing of goats' leather. But this enterprise came to naught because Kieft, a truculent fellow where Indians were concerned, got himself embroiled in a series of small wars with them, and Melyn was forced to flee with his wife and children back to the fort at New Amsterdam.

It was not until 1649 that Melyn found himself in the mood to again return to Staten Island. Kieft, who had proven no help to anyone, had been recalled, and in his place as director-general we now find Peter Stuyvesant, remembered perhaps more for his silver banded wooden leg and for his pear tree than for anything else. Between him and Melyn there was little love lost, for it was the latter who, in the midst of the Indian difficulties, and vexed over the loss of his property on Staten Island, had gone over the head of Stuyvesant, then newly arrived, and taken his grievance directly to Holland. Stuyvesant termed this an act of insubordination and Melyn found himself banished. But at the Hague the West India Company reversed the decree and, vindicated, he returned to America, arriving, as he states, ". . . in New Netherland in front of the Staten Island where, owing to contrary wind and tides, we cast anchor. The people belonging there, joyfully went on land, thanking God for Having been freed from the water and the ship."

Captain David Pietersen De Vries, 1653

Houses, racks, and barns were built. They had brought cattle and plow oxen and they seem to have prospered over a period of five years. He records that ". . . everything began to be abundant on Staten Island, and through God's blessing I began again to recover my losses."

But Stuyvesant, up at Fort Amsterdam, smiled wryly upon being apprised of his enemy's run of luck and expressed the view that the fellow was becoming a trifle too big for his Dutch breeches. So when Melyn sailed up to Manhattan one August day in 1655 in order to transact some business he was arrested and "thrown in a dark hole." He was still there early in September when Stuyvesant, with seven hundred men in seven vessels, sailed out of the harbor for the Delaware River, where they broke up certain Swedish settlements. However, the local Indians, almost two thousand of them, took advantage of the defenseless state of the town to launch an attack. Accomplishing little on Manhattan, they did as much damage as they could at Hoboken and Pavonia, after which they wiped out the settlement on Staten Island. Altogether a hundred colonists were killed and a hundred and fifty held for ransom. This was the Peach War, precipitated by a trigger-happy fellow named Van Dyke having shot a squaw whom he detected in the act of stealing one of his peaches. When the attack began Melyn had been let out of his cell and he hastened to Staten Island and witnessed the destruction of his colony. Discouraged, he abandoned it and later returned to Holland.

So the efforts by the Dutch to locate upon the Island had come to naught, and while it is probable that a few whites lived there during the next five or six years, there was no formal attempt made until subsequent to 1660, during which year a treaty of peace was renewed with chiefs of the Island and adjacent regions. The following year application was made by nineteen Dutch and French settlers for permission to found a community upon Staten Island, and this proved to be the first permanent lodgment. Its location was at the present South Beach, in an area of flat fields which were suitable for the planting of grain; a creek gave access to the lower bay and there was ample pasturage for cattle. It was to this spot that the Rev. Samuel Drisius of New Amsterdam journeyed by boat every two months to preach and to administer the Lord's Supper to the group which probably included Waldenses, survivors of the massacre in Piedmont in 1655, and who had escaped to Holland, subsequently coming to America. The Rev. Drisius, who was past sixty years of age, was selected because of his ability to preach in English and French, as well as in Dutch. His religious fervor outbalanced his physical vigor, and he was compelled finally to abandon the trips, which were "troublesome on account of the great water or bay which must be crossed. . . ." The hamlet remained small, however, as we gather from Governor Stuyvesant's reference to Staten Island in 1666: "It is inhabited only on the south side, behind the hill, and consequently out of sight of the Fort, by ten or twelve men but so and so able to bear arms, who, in order to be protected against a sudden attack of the Savages, did, about a year ago, erect a small slight wooden block house, about eighteen or twenty feet square, in the center of their houses, which were slightly constructed of straw and clapboards."

The settlers were soon to experience a change of rule, for upon accession to the English throne of Charles II the discussions which had begun during Cromwell's protectorate broadened. The British argued that all the "northern" territory, having years previous been discovered by the Cabots, then in England's employ, rightfully belonged to the Crown, and the Dutch had no business there. They admitted that King James may have granted the Dutch an island, later called Staten Island, to use as a watering place for their West India fleets, but royal vouchsafement need not be construed as license to embark upon a spree of wholesale colonization. So Charles II told his brother James, the Duke of York, that he could have as a grant the Dutch occupied territory; he would, however, be obliged to take it away from the Hollanders by force or otherwise.

The Duke, a resourceful man, promptly borrowed four men-of-war and told Colonel Richard Nicolls what he had in mind. Nicolls hoisted sail and put to sea. The Rev. Drisius was an eye-witness to what subsequently took place. He writes on September 8, 1664: "They arrived in the Bay of the North River, near Staten Island, four great men-of-war, or frigates, well manned with sailors and soldiers . . . They landed their soldiers about two leagues from here, at Gravezandt, and marched them over Long Island to the ferry opposite this place. The frigates came up under full sail on the 4th of September with guns trained on one side. They had orders, and intended, if any resistance was shown to them, to give a full broadside on this open place. . . . Our Honorable rulers of the Company, and the municipal authorities of the City, were inclined to defend the place, but found that it was impossible, for the city was not in a defensible condition. And even if fortified, it could not have been defended, because every man posted on the circuit of it would have been four rods distant from his neighbor. Besides the store of powder in the fort, as well as in the city, was small. No relief, or assistance, could be expected, while daily great numbers on foot or on horseback, from New England, joined the English, hotly bent upon plundering the place. Savages and privateers also offered their services against us. Six hundred Northern Indians with one hundred and fifty French privateers, had even an English commission. Therefore upon the earnest request of our citizens and other inhabitants, our authorities found themselves compelled to come to terms. . . ." A company of soldiers took possession of the block house on Staten Island, and the settlers found themselves subjects of a British king.

Colonel Nicolls became governor, and one of his first official acts was to create the shire of Yorkshire, consisting of Long Island, Westchester, and Staten Island. As Yorkshire this region was divided into three districts, or "ridings". Staten Island was included in the West Riding. The Governor changed the name of the fort in Manhattan to Fort James; New Amsterdam became New York. The hamlet on Staten Island he named Dover. Promises of Island land grants were made to his officers, but since these individuals seem to have been

Britton Cottage, New Dorp, built ca. 1678 (now at Richmondtown Restoration). Photograph by C. W. Hunt, 1898. SIHS.

Christopher Billopp House, Tottenville, built ca. 1680. From *A New and Popular Pictorial Description of the United States*, 1853. SIHS.

reluctant to forsake their calling and turn farmer the lands were awarded to actual settlers.

In 1668 Francis Lovelace succeeded Nicolls as governor, and in 1670 he bought the Island from the Indians. The price of real estate had gone up, but it was still a bargain. Lots were laid out by order of the Governor on the north, east, and on the south shore as far as Great Kills, and the surveyors called it "the most commodiosest seate and richest land in America". The one hamlet, Dover, still stood, but it had developed little.

England and Holland were presently again at war and a Dutch fleet sailed into the bay on July 27, 1673 and without bloodshed took over the town. It was but a brief relinquishment, however, for the Hollanders held it only until peace was declared the following year. The new English governor was Sir Edmond Andros. Upon Staten Island the surveying was resumed and by 1679 about one hundred patents had been granted. Captain Christopher Billopp, hero-protagonist in the legend which concerns his circumnavigation of the Island, was one of the patentees, and in the Council Minutes we read that "At a councel August 5, 1675, the Neck of Land Capt. Billopp is upon is judged to bee about thirteen hundred acres". Billopp it probably was who entertained the travellers Jasper Dankers and Peter Sluyter during their three day walk around Staten Island in 1679, and they refer to the Captain's patent on the "west point, where an Englishman lived alone, some distance from the road". Their account of the trip reveals much concerning the natural features of the Island, its flora, fauna, and its human inhabitants, of whom, according to their estimate, there were one hundred families.

At this point in the Island's history, before it had become the county of Richmond, the government consisted of a justice, clerk, a constable, and five overseers, and its court was held in Gravesend, Long Island. But in 1675, "by reason of the Separacon by water", its jurisdiction became self-contained. In 1683, two months after the arrival of the new governor, Thomas Dongan, it became, by an act of the first Provincial Assembly, the County of Richmond, its name being derived from the town and dukedom of the same name in Yorkshire, England. The Governor must have taken a fancy to the Island, for he took title soon thereafter to some fifty-one hundred acres on the Kill van Kull and called it the "Lordshippe or Manner (Manor) of Cassiltowne". Captain Christopher Billopp's grant was at about the same time enlarged to sixteen hundred acres and dignified by the name of "Lordship or Mannor of Bentley". Soon after the Captain had entertained the Messrs. Dankers and Sluyter he seems to have made a trip to England. But he was back on Staten Island in 1681 and in trouble with his neighbors. There was the matter of his "seizure" of thirty-eight negroes, and whatever unpleasantness this may have led to gave birth to the rumor that he was about to dispose of his holdings. However, this trouble blew over just previous to the enlarging of his grant. Still he must have been of a truculent and rancorous disposition, being in 1693 charged with kicking and beating one Bryan, while later, for perhaps some like offense, he was in the Fleet prison in England, in which country he later died.

III

The Sedulous Years

IT WAS in 1683, the year during which Staten Island acquired its status as a county, that the Rev. Petrus Tesschenmacker, first minister of the Reformed Church to be ordained in America, came here to live. We recall how, twenty years earlier, the aging but courageous Samuel Drisius, sixty-three year old pastor of the Dutch Church in New Netherland, braved the rough waters of the bay in order to administer spiritual solace and encouragement to the group of settlers at South Beach, thus constituting the first instance of gospel preaching on the Island. But the Rev. Drisius was dead by 1673, the last three years of his life having been passed in inactivity because of feebleness, so that the few families who lived upon the Island were without pastoral guidance for a considerable time, save for occasional visits by some of the Long Island clergy. There was an attempt made by the English governor to install as minister one Morgan Jones, but an almost unanimous lack of enthusiasm on the part of the Island's inhabitants for this arrangement caused its discontinuance. The antipathy to Mr. Jones may have been occasioned because of his inability to preach in French and Dutch, or his life may have been not above reproach, as intimated by some of the French settlers. But the objection to him lay probably in the fact that few Staten Islanders were adherents of the Church of England. So everyone seemed to be satisfied when the Rev. Tesschenmacker, who "had fixed his thoughts on Staten Island" arrived with goods and chattels to set himself down as a resident, registering his cattle mark and taking up eighty acres of farm land on the south shore. He had, before his ordination, done missionary work in Dutch Guiana and previ-

Church of St. Andrew, Richmond, built 1712. Partially destroyed by fire 1867. Photograph ca. 1866. SIHS.

Winant-Winant House, near Rossville, built ca. 1690. Demolished 1932. Photograph by W. M. Winant, ca. 1907. SIHS.

ous to his arrival on the Island had preached at Kingston, New York. Also he had declined a call to Schenectady. We know little concerning the success of his Island pastorate, but he seems presently to have changed his mind concerning the Schenectady invitation, as he left for that northern frontier shortly after 1685. The decision was not a happy one, for in 1690 his head was split open by a tomahawk during the historic massacre by Frontenac's Indian marauders. Following the Rev. Tesschenmacker's departure there were occasional visits to the Island by preachers from other congregations, among them the Rev. Rudolphus Varick.

We next hear of the arrival, in 1693 or shortly thereafter, of the Rev. David de Bonrepos. He became pastor of the French Church which was built at Green Ridge about 1698. It is probable that, previous to its erection, de Bonrepos preached to the English, French and Dutch in the meeting house which the latter had in 1695 put up in Richmondtown. This building, known as the Voorlezer's House, in which Voorlezer Hendrich Cruser dwelt and in which he at times held forth as lay reader and schoolmaster, still stands, restored by the S. I. Historical Society. It is the oldest known elementary school building in the United States.

The Society for the Propagation of the Gospel in Foreign Parts, often called the Venerable Society, sent from England in 1705 the Rev. Aeneas Mackenzie to found the Church of St. Andrew on Staten Island. Upon arrival here he formulated plans for a building at Richmondtown, meanwhile using the French Church for services. The English Church was completed and dedicated during the summer of 1712 and was, as the Rev. Mackenzie puts it, "a pretty handsome church . . . built of stone." Queen Anne had given the congregation a silver chalice and paten, and the English were quite proud of their new edifice and the royal gifts. So the Rev. David de Bonrepos was left with a steadily diminishing flock, now mostly French, to support the church at Green Ridge. The pastor's demise occurred in 1734. While the approximate site of this building, which stood until some years previous to the Revolution, is known, there is no local record of the manner in which it ceased to exist as a structure.

The Rev. Mackenzie died in 1723 and was followed as church head by the Rev. William Harrison, whose rectorate lasted sixteen years and was then filled by the Rev. Jonathan Arnold, who resigned 1745. Richard Charlton came in 1747 but moved to New York during the turmoil occasioned by the Revolution. He died in 1777. St. Andrew's was badly damaged during the war years, but it was rebuilt and in 1788 the Rev. Richard Channing Moore became its rector. During the twenty years of his ministry the church prospered and the chapel on the north shore, which later (1869) became the Church of the Ascension, was built. David Moore, his son, succeeded him and was rector for forty-eight years.

Shortly subsequent to the opening of St. Andrew's the Dutch, probably yearning for a formal house of worship, built (1716) their Reformed Church in what is now Port Richmond. While many structures of this denomination were octagonal and surmounted with cupolas, this edifice was hexagonal. The Rev. Cornelius Van Santvoord was its pastor from 1718 until 1742, at which time he went to Schenectady. The church was without a regular pastor for some years, but in 1790 the Rev. Peter Stryker occupied its pulpit and continued for four years, followed by a three year incumbency by the Rev. Thomas Kirby. The Rev. Peter J. Van Pelt became

Old Latourette House, Richmond Hill, built ca. 1700. Demolished ca. 1900. Photograph by William H. Mersereau, ca. 1889. SIHS.

Garrett Post House, Holland's Hook, built ca. 1700. Demolished ca. 1960. Photograph by George H. Treadwell, ca. 1899. SIHS.

pastoral head in 1802; his successor in 1835 was the Rev. James Brownlee, whose ministry lasted over a period of sixty years. It was during Dr. Van Pelt's time that the Reformed Dutch Church at Richmondtown, which had been built 1769 and destroyed by the British not long afterward, was rebuilt. This was in 1807 and it continued in use until 1878.

By 1698 the Island's population had grown to seven hundred twenty-seven, of which number ten per cent were slaves. Roads were being laid out, one of the earliest being the thoroughfare which ran from the Watering Place (Tompkinsville) to Billopp's, or, as we now know the route: Van Duzer Street, Richmond Road and Amboy Road to Tottenville. Other early roads are shown on the accompanying map.* Two companies of militia were organized, taxes were levied, a prison was built in Coccles Town (Richmondtown) and the county's castigatory resources augmented soon thereafter by the erection, close to the jail, of a whipping post. The authorities were none too gentle in the matter of prescribing punishment, either, for a slave who had helped himself to a few hens was thrown into a cell for twelve days, the incarceration being preceded by a laying on of twenty-five lashes and, upon release, by ten lashes additional, all "upon ye strip'd and bare back".

Almost all who arrived to engage in business were obliged to have licenses. This legal sanction extended to the erection of grist mills, the establishment of ferries and, of course, the dispensing of strong liquors. One had a choice of thirteen retailers of potables in the year 1717.

There were few Indians remaining upon Staten Island, and these must have been well behaved and probably Chris-

* Map deleted in the revised edition.

tians, for the Rev. Aeneas Mackenzie in 1715 reported having baptized some of them. By 1737 the population of the county was eighteen hundred eighty-nine, of whom three hundred forty-nine were negro slaves, and the inhabitants seem to have been generally peaceful, industrious, and modestly prosperous. J. J. Clute, in his *Annals of Staten Island,* describes domestic life of the period.* In a *History of the Province of New York from the First Discovery to the Year 1732* by William Smith, we learn concerning Richmond County that "The inhabitants are principally Dutch and French. The former have a Church, but the latter having been long without a Minister, resort to an Episcopal Church in Richmond Town, a poor mean village and the only one on the Island."

Houseman House, Westerleigh, built ca. 1700. Photograph by George H. Treadwell, ca. 1899. SIHS.

Peter Kalm, the Swedish naturalist, travelled extensively through the colonies during the middle of the 18th Century, and his journal makes interesting reading. The following excerpt is set down verbatim from the Leng and Davis History:

"Near the inn [in Elizabethtown] where we had passed the night, we were to cross a river, and we were brought over, together with our horses, in a wretched half-rotten ferry. . . . The country was low on both sides of the river, and consisted of meadows. But there was no other hay to be got, than such as commonly grows in swampy grounds; for as the tide comes up in this river, these low plains were sometimes overflowed when the water was high. The people hereabouts are said to be troubled in summer with immense swarms of gnats or mosquitoes, which sting them and their cattle. This was ascribed to the low swampy meadows, on which these insects deposit their eggs, which are afterwards hatched by the heat.

---

*Clute, John J., *Annals of Staten Island,* (N. Y. 1877).

De Hart House, Mariner's Harbor, built ca. 1700. Demolished 1942. Photograph by George H. Treadwell, ca. 1899. SIHS.

"As soon as we had got over the river, we were upon Staten Island, which is quite surrounded with salt water. This is the beginning of the province of New York. Most of the people settled here were Dutchmen, or such as came hither whilst the Dutch were yet in possession of this place. But at present they were scattered among the English and other European inhabitants, and spoke English for the greatest part. The prospect of the country here is extremely pleasing, as it is not so much intercepted by woods, but offers more cultivated fields to view. Hills and vallies still continued, as usual, to change alternately.

"The farms were near each other. Most of the houses were wooden; however, some were built of stone. Near every farm house was an orchard with apple trees. Here, and on the whole journey before, I observed a press for cyder at every farm house, made in different manners, by which the people had already pressed the juice out of the apples, or were just busied with that work. Some people made use of a wheel made of thick oak planks, which turned upon a wooden axis by means of a horse drawing it, much in the same manner as the people do with wood; except that here the wheel runs upon planks. Cherry trees stood along the enclosures round corn fields.

"The corn fields were excellently situated, and either sown with wheat or rye. They had no ditches on their sides, but (as is usual in England) only furrows, drawn at greater or lesser distances from each other.

"In one place we observed a water mill so situated that when the tide flowed, the water ran into a pond, but when it ebbed, the flood gate was drawn up, and the mill driven by the water flowing out of the pond.

"About eight o'clock in the morning we arrived at the place where we were to cross the water in order to come to the town of New York. We left our horses here and went on board the yacht: we were to go eight English miles of sea; however, we landed about eleven o'clock in the morning at New York. We saw a kind of wild ducks in immense quantities upon the water; the people called them blue bills, and they seem to be the same with our Pintal Ducks or Linnaeus's Anasacuta; but they were very shy. On the shore of the continent we saw some very fine sloping corn fields, which at present looked quite green, the corn being already come up. We saw many boats in which the fishermen were busy catching oysters: to this purpose they make use of a kind of rakes with long iron teeth bent inwards; these they used either single, or two tied together in such a manner that the teeth were turned towards each other."

On the last day of May the following year Kalm had occasion to travel from Philadelphia to New York. He sailed up the Delaware River as far as Trenton, thence overland across New Jersey to New Brunswick, where he boarded a boat. He writes: "On coming to the mouth of the river [Raritan] we had a choice of two roads to New York, viz: either within the Staten Island or without it. The inhabitants are determined in their choice by the weather; for when it is stormy and cloudy, or dark, they do not venture to sail without, where the sea itself communicates. We took that course now, it being very pleasant weather; and though we struck on the sands once or twice, yet we got loose again and arrived at New York about nine o'clock . . . cherry trees were planted in great quantities before the farm houses and along the high-roads, from Philadelphia to New Brunswick. . . . On coming to Staten Island . . . I found them very common again, near the gardens. . . . All travellers are allowed to pluck ripe fruit in any garden which they pass by; and not even the most covetous farmer can hinder them from so doing."

Johnson House, New Dorp, built ca. 1740. Demolished ca. 1920. Photograph by William T. Davis, SIHS.

Connor House, Greenridge, built ca. 1770. Demolished ca. 1950. Photograph 1936. SIHS.

We trust that no cantankerous landholder begrudged the observant and worthy Peter the pleasure of plucking a few clusters of fruit from overhanging branches, wherever he happened to be. On the Island it must have been a pleasant practice in the sunny summer months, not only for visitors like Kalm, but for those diligent sons of early settlers who looked with justifiable pride at the fat cattle in their meadows and at the black soil of fallow fields. Here upon their island was abundance of everything necessary for the good life; one need but rise with the sun and perform certain age-old tasks, utilizing the strength and faculties with which the Lord had endowed him. The heady talk of resistance to the mother country took a long time to infiltrate into the minds of people who not only were collectively insular but who were individually dispersed over a large area, and for a number of years they pursued their existences in the normal routine of toil and rest and, upon each seventh day, the raising of their voices in thankfulness to the Creator for the peace and bounty which enveloped them and their children.

A romantic incident which must long have been remembered by our forebears was the investiture with knighthood of General Jeffrey Amherst in the English camp on Staten Island. He was one of the commanders in the army that had defeated the French in the campaigns which resulted in the surrender of their possessions in Canada. On their way homeward several brigades of the victorious army under General Robert Moncton encamped upon the plains at New Dorp, and it was here, in October 1761, in an elaborate ceremony attended by scores of distinguished guests and hundreds of inquisitive, wide-eyed rustics, that the red ribbon and other insignia pertaining to the Order of the Bath were bestowed upon the gallant Amherst. It must have been a colorful and brilliant occasion and, to quote Richard Bayles, Island historian, "Probably Staten Island was never honored with being the scene of a more dignified or important royal ceremony." Following this gala observance Sir Jeffrey left for the city. The regiments which had been encamped upon the Island remained until November, when they went aboard ship, taking with them much of the harvest of local farms, for which they paid with good English gold.

Note: Research undertaken by the author since the foregoing account of Amherst's investiture was written reveals the fact that the ceremony took place at the Watering-Place (Tompkinsville) and not at New Dorp. Amherst, in a letter directed to Cadwallader Colden, and dated 18 July 1761, states his preference for Staten Island as "the most proper place to Encamp [the troops] on," and details Lt. Col. James Robertson to the duty of marking out the encampment. Robertson subsequently issued a bulletin stating that "A Camp is now forming on Staten Island, near the Center of which is the Watering-Place . . . ." Since General Amherst, upon his arrival, made his headquarters at Col. Dungan's [Dongan's] it is hardly likely that he would have done so had his army been encamped halfway down the Island instead of on the extensive glebe lands close by. Dongan's house was on the north shore, just east of the Richmond Terrace-Clove Road junction. It was destroyed by fire in 1878.

IV

*The Revolution**

JUST prior to the Revolution the population of Richmond County numbered almost three thousand, and of this number three hundred were negro slaves. As in every other region in the Colonies, political beliefs were divided. However, mostly farmers and fishermen, the Islanders had little time to waste in wrestling with problems concerning Britain's right to exploitation; there were other more tangible matters to wrestle with—the thousand and one daily tasks which had to be looked to if one was to live. They knew about Lexington and Bunker Hill and the British departure from Boston. There were rumors that the fleet was headed for New York, but a man couldn't stand all day sifting rumors when there was ploughing and sowing to be done; and after working from sun-up to dark one was not often in the mood to tramp several miles just to listen to some noisy fellow holding forth in the tap of the *Rose and Crown* or the *Bull's Head,* and there, like as not, after argument had waxed warm, wind up with a cracked head.

Besides, even if you had soberly scrutinized from all angles the quarrel 'twixt Colonies and mother country, ending with the conviction that independence was the only solution, there was the realization that here on the Island, at least, it was just as well to keep this partiality to yourself and outwardly trim your sails to the prevailing wind, which was strongly Tory. The group which held public office, under the guidance of the County's two most prominent and wealthy men, were the justices, constables, assessors, appraisers and pound masters,

View of the Narrows "between Long Island and Staten Island with our Fleet at Anchor and Lord Howe coming in . . . 12th July 1776." Archibald Robertson drawing (in the collection of the New York Public Library) copied by Loring McMillen. SIHS.

** Revised from the writer's *Staten Island under British Rule, 1776-1783* (S. I., N. Y. 1949).

Lt. Col. Christopher Billopp. Frick Collection.

and to antagonize them gained you nothing. The two leaders were Lt. Col. Christopher Billopp, descendant of the first settler bearing the name, and his father-in-law, Judge Benjamin Seaman. None doubted their loyalty to the King.

There were four Island delegates to the First New York Provincial Congress which met in the city on May 22, 1775. But when the Second Congress met in December the Island was not represented. This show of indifference, added to other manifestations of inimical behavior did not go unnoted, and even George Washington was convinced that no co-operation could be expected from the Staten Islanders, "who, after the fairest professions, have shown themselves our most inveterate enemies."

So when the British fleet, having aboard the army commanded by Gen. William Howe, sailed in through the Narrows early in July 1776, the troops that came ashore found themselves amongst friends. As Howe himself put it, they landed "to the great joy of a most loyal people" and, besides the extended hand of welcome, he was witness to a further expression of their fealty, for they dumped forty pounds worth of Continental paper money upon a huge bonfire, "damning the Congress, and saying they would have nothing more to do with it."

William Howe had served under Wolfe at Quebec during the French and Indian war, and it was during this conflict, in 1758, that his older brother, Lord George Howe, lost his life at Ticonderoga. William succeeded him as member for Nottingham, and at the general election of '74 he told his constituents that he would not accept command of an army that might be sent overseas to fight the colonists. But the King recognized a capable officer when he saw one and, when the time came, in the spring of '75, Howe was notified that he, along with two other distinguished fighting men, Generals John Burgoyne and Henry Clinton, was booked for passage aboard the good ship *Cerebus,* bound for New England. He went with a good grace, presently succeeded Gage, fought the battle of Bunker Hill, got himself starved out of Boston, and here he was on Staten Island with a fine army, waiting for reinforcements in case he had to take New York. However, he was hoping that his brother would arrive with something special up his sleeve in the way of an attractive offer to the Congress and so make this bothersome task unnecessary.

He set himself up in a farm house at New Dorp along with Mrs. Joshua Loring, the Boston lady who had fallen in love with him, and entertained the local notables as well as some others who came over posthaste from New Jersey to offer assistance. They probably had some gay evenings at cards, for Howe had the reputation of being as great a gambler as anyone in the army, while Mrs. Loring was his match. But William Howe knew how to give orders as well as he knew how to give odds. He got his sixty-two hundred troops into tents and huts, and billeted as many as possible with the inhabitants with or without invitation. Loyalists arrived from New Jersey, New York, and Connecticut, some to beg commissions, others to pull strings for friends who desired like favors. Plans were laid to organize a brigade of native adherents to the royal cause with Oliver DeLancy as commander, Cortland Skinner, of Perth Amboy, a colonel, and Christopher Billopp a lieutenant colonel. Young Edward Dongan slipped across from New Jersey to offer his services, never thinking that a bullet from the musket of one of the despised rebels would terminate his existence a year later.

General Cleveland, Howe's chief engineer, galloped over the lanes and highways with a strategic eye cocked for favorable sites upon which to build forts or redoubts. Two of the latter were immediately thrown up at Holland's Hook, opposite the Point at Elizabethtown. They presently went to work erecting redoubts on Richmondtown Hill, overlooking the salt meadows, and at other points along the shores.

Admiral Lord Richard Howe arrived July 12 with well over a hundred ships, and after receiving an uproarious welcome from the Halifax fleet was escorted to headquarters at New Dorp. Here there were further ceremonies, but the guard of honor had hardly marched off the premises before brother William handed him the New York newspaper which contained a reprint of the Declaration of Independence, which William himself had gloomily perused a day or so earlier. Lord Richard, despite the fact that he had come well equipped to fight, had left England in the role of negotiator and mediator. Closer to his heart than anything else was the notion that the colonists could be made to see the error of their ways and return to the fold. He even went, it is said, to the trouble of re-christening some of his transports with the names *Good Intent, Amity's Admonition,* the *Felicity,* the *Three Sisters,* the *Father's Goodwill,* and the *Friendship.* But they were, despite the mediatory purport of names which few patriots were ever to read, bristling with sharp steel bayonets and ballasted with an abundance of ammunition. However, the Admiral wished to make friends with the colonists, and his secretary, Henry Strachey, had the Ministry's proposals for peace locked up in his briefcase, or in its eighteenth century equivalent.

He lost no time in card-playing but sent off a letter to the commanding general of the American army in New York with a flag of truce. It bore the superscription "George Washington, Esquire," and got as far as the guard boat off the Battery, but no farther. He then dispatched one of his staff, Colonel Paterson, up the bay in a barge with another missive. The Colonel got into the Kennedy mansion at 1 Broadway, but when he presented the letter with which he had been entrusted, and which bore upon its surface "George Washington, Esq. Etc. Etc." the tall Virginian declined to accept it. But Paterson, who knew what he was there for, divulged the fact that the brothers Howe were at the moment hovering over Staten Island in the guise of doves with olive branches in their beaks. Those were, naturally, not the Colonel's words, but that was the idea he endeavored to convey. Well, since Washington had as much right to be punctiliously addressed as any other general, and since the Howes were patently resolved not to do so, nothing came of the visit, and presently the British staff was crowding the farmhouse at the head of New Dorp Lane, poring over maps and issuing directives. If the Americans wanted a fight the British could oblige.

Generals Clinton and Cornwallis arrived from the south, where they had accomplished nothing, and with this augmentation the combined fighting ships and transports in the upper and lower bays came to over four hundred. On Staten Island and aboard ship there were over thirty thousand men all armed to the teeth.

This host soon gobbled up everything upon the Island that was edible, then killed all the horses that they could buy or steal and barrelled them for future use. After that they fell back upon the execrable salt pork from the ships, which they loathed, and while waiting for action against the enemy amused themselves by tearing down all the fences for use as firewood.

They roared and rambled drunkenly all over the Island and behaved like an army of satyrs on the rampage. What was lacking in the way of local potables was smuggled over the Kills in the form of raw Jersey applejack. The inhabitants, who some weeks earlier had exhibited such manifest joy over the arrival of the troops, were now praying for a swift deliverance from this plague of human locusts.

Their prayers were soon answered. On August 21 a storm broke that was so severe that even the hardiest redcoat was obliged to remain under cover. And on the 22nd at nine in the morning fifteen thousand men and forty field pieces were ferried across the water and put ashore at Gravesend on Long Island. These were followed by two brigades of von Heister's Hessians, bringing the total to twenty thousand. To face these the Americans had less than eight thousand, the remainder of Washington's army being retained in New York. Four days passed. The momentous 27th dawned, hot and sultry, the British went into action, and in the brackish swamps, atop the hills, and over the fields the battle of Long Island was fought. When, later in the day, rain began to fall and darkness descended, the victorious British stopped for breath and Washington and his exhausted and beaten army found themselves on Brooklyn Heights, with the East River between them and Manhattan. It rained during most of the following day, and on the day which succeeded that—the 29th—the planter from Virginia organized his famous retreat so successfully that at dawn on the 30th, when the now refreshed British took it into their heads to move in and finish off their adversary, he was sitting in the stern of a barge being rowed towards the Whitehall slip by half a dozen tough Marblehead fishermen. He wasn't out of trouble, but he had, with the aid of a Heaven-sent fog, outwitted not only Howe, but had tricked those Fates which had been toying with the notion that the War of the Revolution was to end on an August afternoon.

The British general, having demonstrated to everyone con-cerned that pushing an enemy around was mere child's play to his fighting machine, had himself rowed out to the *Eagle* and, after talking things over with Lord Richard, who still had the bee of pacification buzzing inside his cockaded tricorn, it was decided that one last attempt be made to re-establish peace in the Empire by means less sanguinary than those which necessi-tated the utilization of gunpowder. So General Sullivan, who had been captured in the recent engagement, was sent for, en-lightened concerning what was in the Admiral's mind, then re-leased on parole. He reported to General Washington, who grudgingly consented to his going before the Congress with the latest proposals of Howe. What he told the gentlemen in Philadelphia precipitated a three day debate, and resulted in the election by ballot of a committee consisting of Benjamin Frank-lin, John Adams, and Edward Rutledge to call upon Lord Howe for further discussion.

It was a two day trip to Amboy, whence they were to cross to the Billopp house on Staten Island, and while during the journey much brilliant political conversation must have passed between the three deputies, nothing concerning it seems to have been recorded save Franklin's disquisition on the origins of the common cold, and an account of his difficulty with Adams, who, at a New Brunswick tavern, desired the bedroom window closed, while Franklin desired it open. The latter won, for he talked both Adams and himself to sleep.

Upon reaching Perth Amboy next morning—September 11 —they found Lord Howe's barge tied up to the dock at the foot of Smith Street, along with a senior officer who had been sent to meet the delegates and offer to remain as hostage against their safe return. However, they assured him that this formality was unnecessary and insisted that he return with them in the barge, a complimentary gesture which no end pleased Lord Richard, who stood at the water's edge to greet them. There was a battalion of Hessians drawn up in two lines as a guard of honor, and the party sauntered past the Germans who were, as Adams later reported, "looking fierce as ten Furies, making all the grimaces, and gestures, and motions with their muskets with bayonets fixed, which, I suppose, military etiquette requires, but which we neither understood nor required."

Billopp—he was now a lieutenant colonel of loyalist militia —had for some time been living with his father-in-law, and the degree of order in his former habitation would have aroused no envy in the breast of even the most slatternly housewife. In general the house was, to again quote Adams, "dirty as a stable." But a fatigue detail must have been sent in the previous day to render at least one room presentable, and in it the delegates found a table set with a collation consisting of ham, tongues, mutton and bread, together with a few bottles of excellent claret with which to wash it down. This inelegant and matter-of-fact disposal of the wine must have been anticipated by Howe, since he could hardly have expected the visiting trio to toast the King's health. Spread over the floor was a carpet of green sprigs and moss, which rustic décor did not escape the observing eye of Adams, who vowed it "not only wholesome, but romantically elegant."

The commander of the escort battalion, a Hessian colonel, was invited to sit down with the others and they discussed the comestibles and the claret and probably the weather. But it was not until the meal had ended and the colonel had retired that the conference began.

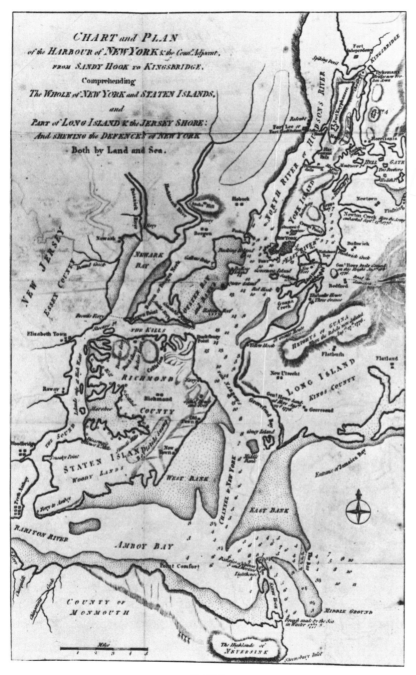

"Chart and Plan of the Harbour of New York,"
1781. SIHS.

Aside from the trip having afforded the three delegates an excuse for almost a week's respite from their congressional duties —and not one of the three had the remotest idea that the powwow at Billopp's would hatch the formula for peace— the conference was a failure. Richard and William Howe, both Whigs, must have been sorely disappointed, the former because he had been sincerely working to effect a reconciliation between America and the mother country; the latter simply because commanding the King's forces in America and being saddled with the responsibility of defeating the colonists was distasteful to him. He had not desired the post in the first place.

So with nothing gained, but marred by not the slightest show of truculence or rancor, the conference ended. His Lordship and his three guests from the City of Brotherly Love walked past the grimacing Hessian guard back to the barge where, with mutual and polite expressions of good-will they parted, and the delegates were rowed across to the Jersey shore and the dock at the foot of Smith Street. It would have been natural for Franklin to dryly remark, when they were out in the stream aways, "At least, gentlemen, one could not cavil at the entertainment!"

There was little more than a brigade of the British remaining on Staten Island, and its people enjoyed an interlude of comparative quiet. They looked ruefully at the holes in the earth where fence posts had recently stood and decided that the absence of barriers made little difference, since there were no cattle save a few which had been secreted in the woods. The poultry was non-existent. As a matter of fact, the animal life upon the Island consisted only of its citizens, who, with winter approaching, thanked their stars for the water all about them, in which there swam an abundance of fish and other edible denizens of the deep.

The main force of the British had for the past fortnight been encamped about Flushing and Newtown on Long Island, presumably awaiting the outcome of the conference. But that last effort to patch matters up was now a thing of the past. On Friday the thirteenth four ships sailed up the East River; others joined them next day; and at eleven o'clock on the morning of the fifteenth this naval force began to pour shot into the American lines at Kip's Bay (34th St.). By nightfall the British were in possession of the city, while Washington was herding his panicky soldiers together on Harlem Heights, pondering upon what one man could do to make an army stand and fight. Well, to his astonishment they did stand and fight next day; they even chased the redcoats back to their lines. There the British remained for four weeks, throwing up earthworks in the pleasant Fall weather and wondering when their commander was going to give them another go at the rebels.

Shortly after one o'clock on the morning of the twenty-first of September a certain tavern keeper who lived near the Watering Place on Staten Island stuck his head out of a bedroom window in order to see if there was any rain in the sky. The weather had been dry—too dry; the wind was from the south. He knew it was from the south because it whistled annoyingly into his right ear. Straight ahead was the east, and before long the sun would be coming up out of the sea back of Long Island. He wondered how the folks there had made out with the British. He himself had done well; they never minded giving up their silver for drink, though there were many who had complained of the soldiers' highhanded methods in regard to other things. The redcoats were in the city now, and business there would be good, better than it had been during the past six months' occupancy by the Americans, who were a poor lot. Lord, he'd give much could he but have even a little bush shop not far from the Fly Market while the British were in town. He cocked an eye towards the north, and what he saw caused him to grip hard on the sill. His heart gave a great leap. Gadamercy, the city was in flames, burning like a field of sun-crisped grain! Everything was going up in smoke by the looks of it—houses, churches, taverns, and even the little bush shops.

During all that night people stood upon the hills to watch the fiery spectacle and wax contentious concerning its origin. Later the British blamed the Americans, while they blamed the British, but the blaze was probably started by some rum-ridden incendiaries. The fire lasted until noon next day, by which time Trinity Church and nearly five hundred other buildings had gone up in flames. Almost the entire town south of St. Paul's Chapel and west of Broad Street lay in ashes.

Three weeks later the King's troops who were stationed on the Island discovered that the enemy across the Kills had no intention of allowing them to gamble, carouse and court the local belles undisturbed. On the night of October fifteen a detachment of Americans crossed the Arthur Kill and by daylight reached a point close to Richmondtown. It is not clear what they had in mind besides stirring up the redcoats in the vicinity of the village, but they did this so effectively that, had not their boats been ready when again they hove into view below Blazing Star, this time with the British at their heels, the entire detail would most likely have been captured. There were three or four killed on each side, some wounded, while all the windows of St. Andrew's were shot out by the Americans before they learned that it was being used as a hospital.

The winter drew on. Washington had crossed the Hudson after a series of set-backs and, desperate and discouraged, was retreating through New Jersey with Cornwallis constantly peppering his rear guard, but managing just in time to get the Delaware River between himself and the enemy. Christmas Day arrived, and Staten Islanders were celebrating as best they could with soldiers billeted in almost every house. Down in Trenton a German brigade was indulging in some real old-country Hochzeit, all warm with rum and blissfully ignorant of the fact that a few hours hence would find them high-tailing it through the icy streets of the town with a lot of tough, yelling, vengeful Americans after them. And when the news of Washington's easy victory reached the Island there must have been quiet rejoicing in more than one local habitation.

During the remainder of the winter there were a few insignificant raids across the Kill van Kull by small parties of hungry British who managed on two occasions to bring back some two score head of cattle and sheep. But the main armies did nothing. Washington had been at Morristown since the first of the year and Howe was in New York, with a sizeable force in New Brunswick and another in Amboy. Early in June Sir William—he had been awarded the Order of the Bath for his victory on Long Island—let it be known that he was setting out by land for Philadelphia and moved his army into a position between Princeton and Morristown endeavoring to bring on a general engagement. But the Virginian, grown foxy, remained where he was in the hills, refusing the bait. Howe withdrew, and with his return to Staten Island the tribulations of that locality began anew. However, this visitation was of short duration, for late in July Sir William got his army and his light-o'love aboard ship and set sail for the Delaware Capes, leaving only a small force to watch the Jersey shores.

They had not long to watch, for early in August a body of Americans under a Major Irving crossed the Kills, landed at Decker's Ferry (Port Richmond), and headed for Rich-mondtown. Now a detachment of troops normally com-manded by a major possessed no great combat power, and why it brashly headed for the center of an island whose shores were well patrolled seems a mystery. They were either just looking for trouble or were itching for another try at the windows of St. Andrew's. They got their wish on both counts, for after having riddled the new panes in the church they were obliged to leg it briskly down the Fresh Kill Road in order to get back to New Jersey with whole skins. As it turned out, the few prisoners they had managed to take were abandoned in a barnyard and a few of their own number killed or wounded.

John Sullivan, the general who had been captured in the battle of Long Island and who later covered himself with glory at Trenton, having got wind that the British on the Island were rather thinly spread out, then decided to try his hand at an invasion. Accordingly, with a force of fifteen hundred in two detachments, he landed at two separate points late on the night of the twenty-first of August and engaged in a confused and complicated series of encounters which, accord-ing to published reports, seem to have taken place over most of the Island and the waters thereof. All seemed to agree that the invaders burned some thirty-five tons of hay and a barn near Decker's Ferry. Sullivan states that he "put to rout six regiments; killed, wounded and made prisoners of at least four or five hundred of the enemy . . . lost not more than a hundred and fifty men." The British claimed that "a con-siderable number of the enemy were killed and about three hundred taken prisoners." However, regardless of whose was the victory, this action was only a summer night's appetizer for John Sullivan, for three weeks later he was mixed up with Cornwallis in a man's-size fight at Brandywine Creek. The General never sat on the side lines if he could manage to get into a tussle with an adversary.

With the exception of several minor raids by both sides across the Kills during the month of November, things were quiet on the Island. Winter laid its icy grip upon the land—it was the terrible year of Valley Forge—and the only ones who had a gay time were the British in Philadelphia. Sir William Howe, who had asked to be relieved of his command, lived in a fine house, attended concerts and balls, still enjoying the company of Mrs. Loring. It was May of 1778 when Sir Henry Clinton took over command of the British army in America, and Sir William sailed for home, leaving his erstwhile lady friend to play cards with whom she chose, and himself not too unhappy over having bungled a job for which he had felt only detestation.

Local tongues were set wagging over the capture of Colonel Billopp, who on a night early in June attended a ball in the home of a patriot lady of Blazing Star whom everyone, including the Colonel, took to be a Loyalist. She had a brother in Woodbridge, one Captain Fitz Randolph, who, hearing of the event and learning, perhaps from the lady herself, that Billopp would be present, decided that he would attempt to bag the prominent Tory. He crossed from New Jersey with fifteen companions and while they waited in a thicket he proceeded to his sister's house. There, sure enough, was the Colonel, disporting himself in a new dance called an Allemando, and to all appearances thoroughly enjoying himself. So Fitz Randolph, having marked his man, helped himself to a glass of Madeira from a proffered tray and departed. Billopp, during the course of the evening, had also helped himself, liberally, no doubt, as was the custom. He and a companion, riding drowsily homeward, reins slack and chins drooping into their cravats, were almost unseated when their horses suddenly shied, and the two Tories found themselves prisoners of Fitz Randolph and his party. The bold captain from Woodbridge scooped up a few sleepy sentinels on his way to the boats and they crossed to the other side. Two months later Billopp was exchanged and returned to his home.

Apparently the friends of Colonel Billopp resented his late capture and incarceration and in February of 1779 a party of the new Levies went across to Woodbridge and nabbed the gallant Fitz. The captain was forced to remain in British custody until fifteen months later, when he was exchanged for a Captain Jones.

But to match this exploit the Americans again captured Billopp. The steeple of St. Peter's Church in Perth Amboy proved to be an excellent lookout point for watchers who could, by means of a telescope, check the identity of anyone who chanced to be strolling about the grounds of Billopp's house across the water. When, after days of observation, they detected the Colonel taking the air of an afternoon, they organized their party. It was June 23, 1779, and as dark as a night could be when they rowed across to the Island shore with muffled oars. They possessed the countersign but no one challenged them, and they hustled Billopp out of his bed and into a boat. It was December 26 before he was liberated from the jail at Burlington.

The weather which followed was so cold and stormy that it was remembered as the "hard winter," and there was price fixing of cordwood, upland and salt hay, straw, Indian corn and grains. The Kills were frozen over, as well as the East and Hudson Rivers.

With easy access to the Island thus provided by the elements, General Stirling decided to try his luck in an attack. Heretofore his luck had not been of the best, and upon this occasion it proved to be no better. The night, January 14, 1780, was unusually cold and the snow was waist deep; the twenty-five hundred men who comprised the invading force suffered intensely. After he had got his troops on to the Island, Stirling learned that his visit was, contrary to what he had planned, no surprise to the British. So he halted in his tracks, set his men to building huge fires of cordwood which were expediently nearby, and waited for dawn. But then, having ascertained that the enemy had dispatched a boat to the city with a call for reinforcements, he waited around until further scouting convinced him that an assault would be disastrous, and early on the morning of the 16th recrossed to Elizabeth Town. As if the cup of tribulation of the local civilians had not previously been caused to sufficiently overflow by reason of British and Hessian plundering, they had to endure more of the same treatment from Stirling's soldiers, aided and abetted by Jersey opportunists. So manifest and manifold were the evidences of this large scale and sudden onslaught upon the unfortunate residents that Stirling caused his troops to be searched when they had recrossed the frozen Kill van Kull and, with the help of Elizabeth Town's Rev. Caldwell, much of the loot was returned to its rightful owners. This was the last incursion of any magnitude, but there was no cessation of petty violence for many months.

Cornwallis surrendered at Yorktown on the 19th of October, 1781, but it was not until December 5, 1783, that the last of the British army left Staten Island. A little over a week previous to this the greater part of it had sailed homewards through the Narrows, to the great joy of the hundreds who

stood upon the heights where the enemy had built a huge re-
doubt, partly of timbers cut from adjacent forest land. But it
was not until the last of the Island garrison had got aboard the
transport which lay offshore at the Watering Place, and the
Ceres, upon which was Sir Guy Carleton, last of King
George's commanders in America, had hoisted sail that the
people could believe that the destiny of America was wholly
in their hands. Their forests were all but ruined; their live
stock was almost non-existent; churches as well as dwellings
were but charred ruins. But the land was freed, the armies
had departed, and the pleasant sunshine fell upon bodies that,
despite deprivations, were still sound and sturdy. The country would grow; their children would grow with it, each generation a little better than the one which had gone before. They
were free citizens of a free America, as of this December day
and hour. The Declaration had been a brave, resolute promise;
this was triumphant fulfillment.

V

Hamlets Into Villages

THERE was nothing cataclysmic in the transition to a republican form of government; the Island was still a county with county officials. There were scars and bruises all about, to be sure, but foundations were still firm, even though the habitations which had stood upon them were in ruins. Boundary lines were for the most part apparent, despite the disappearance of fences. And beneath the rank growth of weeds was the fertile soil, ready to transmute its riches into abundant harvests.

The two most prominent Loyalists, Christopher Billopp and Benjamin Seaman, had departed for Canada, along with several thousands from other localities who had been actively antagonistic to the patriot cause, and their property, forfeited to the people of the State of New York, was sold.

The ruined court house in the county seat, Richmondtown, was levelled to its foundations and a new structure built (1792) nearby on the Fresh Kill Road. Public stocks were erected close by for citizens who were in need of mild chastisement. The Church of St. Andrew, by now in a deplorable state, was repaired, and the Reformed Dutch Church at Port Richmond, which had been destroyed while the British were in possession of the Island, was rebuilt, as was the little church of the same denomination at the county seat.

Socially, matters were much as they had previously been. In contrast to the city across the bay, Staten Island's population had been cut to one pattern. There was no aristocratic class, nor were there many professional men or well-to-do merchants. The three thousand Islanders who, upon the eve of

Clauson House, New Dorp, built ca. 1795. Demolished 1946. Photograph by C. Sykes, 1936. SIHS.

the Revolution, found themselves searching their hearts and minds for an answer to the burning question concerning how their loyalty was to be bestowed quickly discovered in 1776 that they had better shout for the King; with thirty thousand British troops upon the doorstep it was the thing to do. For the entire seven years of the war's duration no civilian had been obliged to strain his eyesight for the glimpse of a redcoat. And when the curtain at length descended on the departing *Ceres* people knew that when again it rose it would be they who would be moving about upon the newly set stage with all the world as audience.

So old animosities were perforce soon forgotten, and they rebuilt their houses, their churches, and their mills. A number of British soldiers had deserted previous to the departure of their regiments, and these were added to the population. Folks went about their daily affairs. Cornelius Dissosway rebuilt his mill in 1800, purchasing one hundred shingles from Jacob Winant and three thousand hard and soft brick from Thomas Acorn. The mill dam required the utilization of a scow, and this was hired from Abraham Woglom. William Wood provided floodgates, while planks were furnished by Joseph Wright. It must have been a chilly operation, however, for Dissosway's records show a receipt from a man named Butler "for rum he had for building the mill." The mill owner was under considerable other expense, too, during the same period, for he paid Isaac Stuart and Godfrey Sweeny tuition for the schooling of three young Dissosways, as well as a fee of one pound ten shillings to a physician who vaccinated three Negro children.

The property which Governor Dongan had owned had been divided and sold. The immense Billopp estate in the southern part of the Island was broken up, as well as the lands belonging to Benjamin Seaman. The Glebe, a farm of three hundred forty acres which in 1718 had been bequeathed to St. Andrew's Church by Elias Duxbury diminished in extent when the State took thirty acres in 1799 for the establishment of a lazaretto, or quarantine for persons infected with yellow fever and other contagious diseases. Five acres of this parcel were later conveyed to the Federal Government and it is this land which is at the present time used by the U. S. Coast Guard. Staten Islanders, having not long before got rid of one obnoxious pest, the British army, did not welcome this even more deadly menace to their well-being. But their protests were unavailing; they got the lazaretto and its infected inmates, which no one else wanted. And since contagion had no respect for the high walls which shut in the buildings of the reservation they also got yellow fever. During the first year of the institution's operation there were twenty-five extra-mural cases of this pestilence. But fifty-nine years elapsed before the inhabitants, weary of protesting, organized a raid upon the place and burned it.

By the year 1800, with Staten-Island's population numbering four thousand five hundred and sixty-four, one might rightly conclude that it remained a region of wide open spaces. By the end of the next decade nearly a thousand additional individuals had arrived, and when war again broke out in 1812 the Island was still largely an agricultural community. Daniel D. Tompkins was at the time Governor of the State and it was his urging which had resulted in the erection of fortifications at the Narrows, mere earthworks, but with emplacements for a formidable array of ordnance. Defenses of a similar kind were constructed at Prince Bay, while upon Pavilion Hill the old British fort was overhauled and a few cannon set up. The local militia were activated, and towards the end of the war the troops detailed to duty on the Island consisted of a brigade of two thousand one hundred and fifty officers and

Pierson House, Mariner's Harbor, built ca. 1780. Demolished. Photograph ca. 1895. SIHS.

Daniel Tompkins, by J. W. Jarvis. Engraved by T. Woolnoth. SIHS.

men. Cannon of various caliber which had been put in readiness for the defense of Long Island, Manhattan, and Staten Island numbered more than nine hundred. The personnel which manned this vast assortment of artillery consisted of the militia and volunteer regiments, but everyone who could handle a spade had helped in the digging, even children. However, the British never got close enough to test this panoplied area and the panicky but resolute New Yorkers put on a big celebration when in February 1815 news arrived that the war was over. The guns at the Narrows went off in a mighty roar of thanksgiving, there followed a "feu de joie" by the infantry, and an extra ration of rum was issued to all concerned.

Governor Tompkins was born in Westchester County in 1774 and died on Staten Island in 1825. He was elected governor of New York in 1807 and served until elected vice-president in 1817. It was he who was responsible for the development of Tompkinsville, having in 1815 bought most of the Duxbury Glebe land. Several of the streets still bear the names of his children: Arietta, Minthorne, and Hannah. His son Minthorne, along with W. J. Staples, was active in the development of Stapleton in 1833. The Governor procured in 1816 the incorporation of the Richmond Turnpike Company, resulting in the construction of a highway bearing that name which spanned the Island from Tompkinsville to Travis, having for its purpose the shortening of the stage route between New York and Philadelphia. It started from Duxbury Street at the Quarantine and ended at the "Jersey warfe" after having passed a "black walnut sapling . . . near the edge of the salt marsh". This thoroughfare, formerly named Richmond Turnpike, was once a rural road bordered with post and rail fence and woodland. Today, starched with concrete, it bears the commemorative name of Victory Boulevard. In 1816 the Governor bought an interest in the steamboat enterprises of Livingston and Fulton, and was also owner or part-owner of the *Nautilus,* one of the boats which plied between the Island and New York.

Barrett Nephews Dye Works, 1885. SIHS.

Staten Island began to lose its strictly rural aspect during the next few years. The section which we now know as West New Brighton was once known as Factoryville and it was here, in 1819, that the firm of Barrett and Tileson established their Dyeing and Printing Company which, once fully in operation, employed over one hundred workmen. Their business was the dyeing and printing of fabrics, and many of those who were on the company's rolls had come from New England, experienced men in the textile arts.

Oysters had always been plentiful off the Island shores, especially at Mariners' Harbor and in the vicinity of Tottenville. With an ever increasing commerce in this popular article of diet came a demand for improved means of transport, so small shipyards were started and iron workers settled nearby. There was established in 1833 a gun factory in New Brighton which two years later moved to the Willowbrook area. A flour mill, brickyards, a factory which produced wall paper, and another which processed whale oil were erected and put into operation. In 1833 the mining of iron was undertaken, much of the product destined for the manufacture of red ochre paint, the principal scenes of this activity being at the southern end of Jewett Avenue, upon Todt Hill, and on Ocean Terrace.

While the famous institution known as Sailors Snug Harbor was founded in 1801 by Captain Robert Randall, it was not until 1831 that the site now occupied by the thirty

Fiedler House, New Brighton, built ca. 1835. Demolished. Photograph by Charles G. Hine, 1912. SIHS.

Ward House (Cement House), New Brighton, built ca. 1837. Demolished 1920. Photograph by George H. Treadwell, 1899. SIHS.

or more buildings was purchased. The Captain had done a bit of privateering in the days when there was no opprobrium attached to the calling, and had in 1790 invested part of his fortune in twenty-one acres of farm land in Manhattan. His will stipulated that this, together with the mansion which stood upon it be used as a home for "aged, decrepit, and worn-out sailors". The trustees of the estate, all farsighted gentlemen, leased the Manhattan property to commercial interests and established the home on Staten Island. Here the retired mariners swap yarns, whittle ship models, and sit in the sunshine. The bronze statue of Captain Randall which faces the water is the work of Augustus St. Gaudens and was unveiled in 1884.

What were once small clusters of dwellings were now villages. A son of the Governor, Minthorne Tompkins, in association with William J. Staples, bought, in 1833, land on the East Shore from Cornelius Vanderbilt and his brothers and sisters. Three years later this area had attained the status of a village and the promoters, proud of their project, saw fit to celebrate its baptism. Prominent citizens were recipients of the following invitation: "The Inhabitants of the vicinity of the New Ferry, Staten Island, having given the name of 'Stapleton' to that neighborhood; Messrs. Tompkins and Staples request the pleasure of the company of yourself and friends at 8 o'clock on Saturday Evening, the 23rd Inst. at the Bay House, in commemoration of the event. July 19th, 1836."

Of New Brighton, a prospectus of the same year states that it "combines advantages which, it is believed, are unrivalled in this country. Added to its proximity to the great commercial mart of the western hemisphere, it possesses a

Whitehall, South, and Staten Island Ferries. From *Gleason's Pictorial Drawing-Room Companion,* September 24, 1853. SIHS.

"*New Brighton From New York Bay, Engraved and published for the New Brighton Mirror,*" 1838. Engraved by Rolph. SIHS.

Old Place Mill, Old Place, built ca. 1804. Demolished. Photograph by C. W. Hunt, 1893. SIHS.

beauty of location, extent of prospect, and salubrity of climate that will in vain be sought elsewhere. . . . It is separated from the City of New York by a distance of only five miles, which will be traversed throughout the day by two swift and beautiful steamboats . . . in a period of twenty minutes . . . it is worthy of remark that these shores are uniformly free from the deposit of nuisance of any kind . . . fish and game of various descriptions are to be found in every direction".

Samuel Akerly wrote in 1842: "the whole eastern shore is becoming almost a continued village from the Quarantine [Tompkinsville] to the Signal poles at Fort Richmond being occupied by country seats and town plots. . . . The north side of Staten Island is more thickly inhabited than any other part; and for several miles is one continued settlement or succession of villages . . . the road along the kills is thickly studded with elegant mansions . . . for a mile or more westward of Port Richmond, the road along the kill continues thickly inhabited by persons engaged in the boating, bathing and oyster trade".

James Stuart, in his *Three Years in America,* describes the rural areas of the Island in 1829 as follows: "We had a fine drive through the most interesting parts of the island, the surface of which is much varied. We saw many comfortable-looking farm houses, amidst rich valleys and lands, and orchards abounding in fruit; but what most surprised me in looking at the fruit, was the extraordinary quantity of cherry trees producing the small black and red cherry. In this ride, I saw a greater number of cherry trees, I am persuaded, than I had seen in the whole course of my life. . . . No part of the wood in Staten Island . . . is of great size, the British during their occupation of New York, in the revolutionary war, having cut down for fuel all the wood within their reach."

Peter Kalm was not, apparently, the only visitor who admired our cherry trees.

Henry David Thoreau lived as tutor at the home of Judge William Emerson on Emerson Hill from May to October, 1843. The famous naturalist, then twenty-six years of age, enjoyed the Island's rural charm, for of his observations, during the first month of his sojourn, he writes:

Johnson House, Elm Park, built before 1800, altered ca. 1840. Demolished ca. 1940. Photograph by Eugene G. Putnam, ca. 1900. SIHS.

"I have already run over no small part of the island, to the highest hill, and some way along the shore. From the hill directly behind the house I can see New York, Brooklyn, Long Island, the Narrows, through which vessels bound to and from all parts of the world chiefly pass—Sandy Hook and the Highlands of Neversink (part of the coast of New Jersey)—and, by going still farther up the hill, the Kill van Kull, and Newark Bay. From the pinnacle of one Madame Grimes' house, the other night at sunset, I could see almost round the island. Far in the horizon there was a fleet of sloops bound up the Hudson, which seemed to be going over the edge of the earth; and in view of these trading ships, commerce seems quite imposing. But it is rather derogatory that your dwelling-place should be only a neighborhood to a great city—to live on an inclined plane. I do not like their cities and forts, with their morning and evening guns, and sails flapping in one's eye. I want a whole continent to breathe in, and a good deal of solitude and silence, such as all Wall Street cannot buy—nor Broadway with its wooden pavement. I must live along the beach, on the southern shore, which looks directly out to sea, and see what that great parade of water means, that dashes and roars, and has not yet wet me, as long as I have lived".

A week later he wrote: "The cedar seems to be one of the most common trees here, and the fields are very fragrant

New York Bay from the Telegraph Station,
1838. Drawn by W. H. Bartlett and engraved by
R. Wallis, London, 1838. SIHS.

New York Bay from the Narrows, after 1865.
Drawn by F. B. Schell and engraved by C. H.
Smith. SIHS.

with it. There are also the gum and tulip trees. The latter
is not very common, but it is very large and beautiful, having
flowers as large as tulips, and as handsome. It is not time for
it yet. The woods are now full of a large honeysuckle in full
bloom, which differs from ours in being red instead of white,
so that at first I did not know its genus. The painted cup is
very common in the meadows here. Peaches, and especially
cherries, seem to grow by all the fences. Things are very
forward here compared with Concord [Massachusetts]. The
apricots growing out of doors are already as large as plums.
The apple, pear, peach, cherry, and plum trees have shed their
blossoms. The whole island is like a garden, and affords very
fine scenery. In front of the house is a very extensive wood,
beyond which is the sea, whose roar I can hear all night long,
when there is a wind; if easterly winds have prevailed on the
Atlantic. There are always some vessels in sight—ten, twenty,
or thirty miles off—and Sunday before last there were hundreds in long procession, stretching from New York to Sandy
Hook, and far beyond, for Sunday is a lucky day. I went to
New York Saturday before last. A walk of half an hour, by
half a dozen houses along the Richmond Road . . . brings me
to the village of Stapleton, in Southfield, where is the lower
dock; but if I prefer I can walk along the shore three quarters
of a mile farther toward New York to the quarantine village
of Castleton, to the upper dock, which the boat leaves five or
six times every day, a quarter of an hour later than the former
place. Farther on is the village of New Brighton, and farther
still Port Richmond, which villages another steamboat visits.
. . . I have just come from the beach and I like it very much.
Everything there is on a grand and generous scale—seaweed,
water, and sand; and even the dead fishes, horses and hogs
have a rank, luxuriant odor; great shad-nets spread to dry;

crabs and horseshoes crawling over the sand; clumsy boats, only for service, dancing like sea-fowl over the surf, and ships afar off going about their business".

Up to that period when the first steam ferry was put into operation the Island's transportation had been of a rather primitive type. Three hundred years ago, if one of Melyn's colonists had been of a mind to cross the Kill van Kull in order to do a little trading with the Jersey Indians, he would have been obliged to fish a bit of wampum out of his pocket in payment for passage in a canoe or rowboat. These were long utilized for the transportation of individuals across the narrow Kills, but for the rougher trip up the bay the small sloop was in demand. Flatboats which were propelled by oars and often by means of a square sail accommodated a number of passengers as well as animals and were called periaguas. A variation of this craft was the horse-boat, which employed a horse-operated treadle connected with side wheels. These scow-like boats were still in use more than ten years subsequent to the advent of steam ferries.

In 1812 the largest and fastest periagua in the bay was commanded by Capt. Cornelius Vanderbilt, then eighteen years of age, who, five years later, became interested in steam transportation. He ran a steamboat between New York and New Brunswick, where he lived until 1829. He then moved to Stapleton, making his home in a modest dwelling on land now occupied by the Paramount Theatre. Later he built an imposing house on ground nearby.

Robert Fulton made his famous trip up the Hudson in 1807. But it was ten years later that the steamboat *Nautilus* began to make regular trips between Whitehall Street and the Quarantine Landing at Tompkinsville. By 1823 another boat

Cornelius Vanderbilt. Engraving, 1875. SIHS.

Vanderbilt Cottage, Stapleton, built ca. 1790. Demolished ca. 1922. Birthplace of Cornelius Vanderbilt. Photograph by Eugene G. Putnam, ca. 1900. SIHS.

Village of Richmond. Oil on canvas by C. Winter, 1851. Staten Island Institute of Arts and Sciences.

was running between New York and Port Richmond. James Stuart, he of the three year sojourn, undertook the former passage in June, 1829, and our present day commuters must envy him his experience. Regarding the journey he writes:

"While we were enjoying the scene, one of my fellow travellers reminded us, that we must not leave the boat without visiting the bar-room, where we should find everything very nice. Thither we accordingly went. The bar and Gentlemen's cabin contained a great variety of eatables and drinkables such as Bologna sausages, hung-beef, biscuits, and all sorts of confectionary; with wines, spirits, oranges, lemons, limes, lemonade, and ice, which is always to be had in this country. My companions partook of a sausage, and a little brandy and water and sugar, mixed by the bar-keeper, in small tumblers. I had some lemonade. . . . We landed at the quarantine ground in about half an hour. . . . The shores of Staten Island are finely indented, and sprinkled with the white, clean looking villas of this country".

The cost of a one-way passage aboard this 1829 luxury liner was 12½ cents, seemingly a low price for so enchanting a set-up. There were five trips each day, starting at 7 a. m. and if you lived in Richmondtown, the county seat, there was a stage which left the village at 8 a. m. and connected with the 9:30 boat.

Stuart must have proceeded to Pavilion Hill shortly following his arrival, and liking that spot, too, he makes this comment: "Behind the village [Tompkinsville] the ground becomes abrupt, to a point at which a building is erected called the Pavilion, expressly on account of the splendor of the view, the top of which is, I should think, nearly 250 feet above the sea, consisting of handsome saloons, with balconies, piazzas, &c on

Second County Corthouse, Richmond, built ca. 1794; portico added later. Burned 1945. SIHS.

Old Red Jail, Richmond, built ca. 1729. Burned 1895. SIHS.

Old Rossville Hotel, Rossville, built ca. 1829. Demolished ca. 1935. Photograph by George H. Treadwell, ca. 1899. SIHS.

Pavilion Hotel, New Brighton, built ca. 1826. Demolished after 1900. SIHS.

St. James Hotel, Port Richmond, built ca. 1787 with later additions. Demolished 1946. SIHS.

all sides, and a lookout place from the summit, from which the prospect is most glorious. . . . After enjoying the delights of this charming spot for some time, a hint was given, that a visit at the bar-room would be expected." Whether he ordered lemonade this time does not appear.

Later, when Stuart took the "fine drive through the most interesting parts of the island" he and his convivial companions probably stopped at one or more of the taverns along the way. The *Bull's Head,* famous as a meeting place for Tories during the Revolution was still dispensing good cheer. So was the *Black Horse* at New Dorp. The *Old Track House* and the *Old Club House,* both misleading as to name, had just been built at Oakwood, while the *Planters Hotel,* still standing, but bare as to pantry and cellar, was in process of construction on Bay Street. The party probably viewed the beautiful new classic structure which overlooked the water at New Brighton, but if they quenched their thirsts within its walls it was only at the invitation of the occupant, Mr. Thomas E. Davis, for it was not until shortly after 1832 that it became the famous and fashionable Pavilion Hotel.

Third County Courthouse, and Jail, Richmond. Courthouse built 1837. Jail built 1860, demolished 1906. Ca. 1890. SIHS.

VI

Burning of the Quarantine

WITH an increase in population which proximity to New York made inevitable, the Island steadily developed. Many small businesses were begun which served their generation; some few are today flourishing enterprises. While these modest but solid citizens were pursuing village existences and serving their fellow-townsmen to the best of their abilities, others, farseeing and ambitious, were conceiving broader projects. Men talked of building a steam railroad and effecting improvements in the services of the various ferries. Robbin's Reef lighthouse was placed in commission (1839). Several newspapers were being published. Volunteer fire companies were organized in every town. Land on Grymes' Hill began to be bought up by well-to-do newcomers and developed into attractive and spacious estates, while others built large mansions in the Bard Avenue section.

There were an incredibly large number of private schools established during the middle 1800's, all hoping to receive support and encouragement from the many individuals of means who had taken up their abode here. The newspapers of the period contain notices of these institutions, but most seem to have enjoyed but brief existences. There were seminaries for young ladies, boarding schools for young gentlemen, a "Classical and Military Academy" presided over by one Major Duff, singing schools and schools for dancing, a "Female Institute," schools which specialized in the teaching of foreign languages, kindergartens, a gymnasium run by a blind gentleman.

The public school system was set up during the administration of Governor Tompkins, although the University of the State of New York had been established in 1784. Early dis-

Destruction of the Quarantine buildings near Tompkinsville. From Frank Leslie's Illustrated Newspaper, September 18, 1858. SIHS.

Ferryboat "Josephine." Photograph by H. Hoyer, ca. 1859. SIHS.

trict schools were supported by local taxes and we read that in 1822 the citizens of Westfield met at John Mersereau's inn and voted two hundred dollars by tax to build a schoolhouse eighteen by twenty feet. But public schools as we now know them date back to the year 1842, when the State made each county or city a unit authorized to raise the necessary funds for free education by taxation. It was at this time that qualifications for teachers and courses of study were standardized.

Four breweries were established during the 1850's. In 1851 the Dye Works, head of which was Nathan Barrett, began business. The following year saw the removal from New York to the Island of the DeJonge paper factory. The Richmond County Mutual Fire Insurance Company was organized in 1836.

During the five years, 1847-51, more than one million immigrants landed at the port of New York. Of these several thousand came to live on Staten Island, some in the farming areas, but most of them close to the factories. These people, dissatisfied with existence in their native lands, their ambitions calibrated to high hopes of better futures for themselves and their children, had been at sea for six weeks, jammed together in steerage quarters where ventilation was almost non-existent and ill health prevalent. The food was inadequate and often spoiled, drinking water stale, while maintenance of personal cleanliness was impossible. Every sailing ship which held passengers ill with contagious or infectious diseases anchored off the Quarantine grounds at Tompkinsville and remained there until all those afflicted were removed to the hospitals. There were no restrictions placed upon the movements of nurses and attendants, who went in and out of the reservation at will to mingle with the general population in nearby villages or travelled back and forth upon the ferryboats which docked nearby. The inevitable result was a steady increase in the "outside" rate of disease.

In 1848, with one hundred and eighty cases of infection amongst townspeople, the alarmed and indignant citizens petitioned the Legislature for relief. A committee was appointed which furnished a lengthy report, ending with the recommendation that the menace be abolished. In April of 1849 the Legislature passed an act which provided for transference of the Quarantine hospitals to Sandy Hook. But New Jersey desired no part of so unpalatable an enterprise, and this antagonism, together with the dereliction of those politicians whose business it was to effect the removal, resulted in nothing being accomplished.

Further protest was made in 1856, and subsequently a farm and buildings were purchased at Seguine's Point, Prince Bay, as a temporary site for the lazaretto, an expedient which was to serve until the Commission was able to find a permanent and isolated location. But the peppery citizens of the south end of the Island burned the buildings and thus put a sudden and spectacular end to that particular project. This summary act convinced the North and East Shore folks that something of the same sort had better be done in regard to the original installation which was still infecting the adjacent community; that so far as the Port authorities were concerned, the mephitic and insalubrious plague spot was likely to fester in their midst until the crack of doom.

The night of Sept. 1, 1858 was warm and pleasant, and each of the thirty men who had assembled for a final briefing beneath the tree on Fort Hill knew exactly what he was to do. All were gentlemen of prominence; all were dedicated to the perpetration of an act of large scale vandalism. None deceived himself with the notion that those who were responsible for the maintenance of law and order would attach a euphemistic label to the deed. On the contrary, all realized that there would be a terrific hullabaloo and that the wrath of authority would descend upon them. However, the bundles of straw were piled nearby, along with an assortment of bottles containing camphene. There was a box of matches for each man. So, dismissing all fears of impending retribution, they went about the business for which they had assembled, their chairman having before dismissing them taken the precaution to read a communication from the local Board of Health, in which the nuisance caused by the presence of the hospitals was termed unbearable, and directing its removal.

They helped themselves to straw, camphene, and matches and made their way to the wall at the upper end of the Quarantine area. This wall was of brick and too high for easy scaling. But someone had thoughtfully deposited a load of beams close to the spot first reached by the East Shore gentlemen. It took no time at all, since the beams had been equipped with handles, for someone to hit upon the idea of utilizing them as battering rams. Presently there was a hole in the wall large enough to admit the entire delegation. Dr. Frederick Hollick, upon whose property the combustibles had been dumped, writes: "There were numerous buildings about the place, many unoccupied, and these were soon on fire. The large hospital for the men, with the wooden statue of a sailor on top, was the next, after it had been cleared of everything, even to a cat and a canary bird. There were only three yellow fever patients, and these were carefully carried out and placed on beds under an open shed, for it was a very warm night, and they laid enjoying the sight, and being well attended to. I believe they all recovered, and no one was taken sick from being in contact with them."

View of the Quarantine and New York harbor from Pavilion Hill. Drawn by E. W. Clay and engraved by J. A. Rolph, 1838. SIHS.

View of the Quarantine grounds and buildings. From *Frank Leslie's Illustrated Newspaper*, September 13, 1856. SIHS.

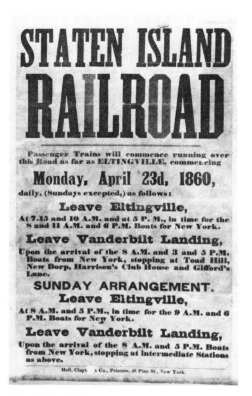

Broadside. SIHS.

First Train out of Tottenville, June 1, 1860.
SIHS.

The glare in the sky attracted many people; the fire engines arrived, but the firemen, after some argument with the gate-keeper, found that someone had slashed their hose, so stood about to observe the conflagration. A few buildings which survived this first invasion were burned the following night.

There followed a retaliatory gesture on the part of the authorities. The wall was mended; temporary buildings were erected in the area; a regiment of militia was detailed to establish martial law in the neighborhood and guard the place. The press dramatized the incident, characterizing those who had been involved in the affair as incarnate fiends, sepoys, savages, and barbarians. The thirty arsonists congratulated each other over their port wine and agreed that the job had been carried out as per schedule. The matter was aired in the courts, but there were no convictions. An old ship was turned into a hospital for the reception of contagious diseases and anchored in the lower bay. Subsequently hospitals were built upon the artificial islands—Hoffman and Swinbourne—off the south shore.

But Staten Islanders were forced to pay for the unconventional manner in which they had rid themselves of the lazaretto. Damage sustained by the State was estimated at one hundred thirty-three thousand eight hundred and twenty-two dollars and the county Supervisors issued bonds to meet this demand, proceeds of the sale of which were devoted to the activities of the Commissioners of Emigration. If there was a sting to this chastisement, its severity was tempered by the conviction that a grave menace to the community had been removed.

The year 1860 also saw the formal opening of the steam railroad on June 2. Trains drawn by wood burning locomotives ran from Vanderbilt's Landing (Clifton) to Tottenville five times a day, with connections for New York by way of the ferryboats *Westfield* and *Clifton*. Telegraphic connection between the Island and New York also was established. Stages ran from Richmondtown to the Vanderbilt Landing and to Port Richmond. The steamboats *Flora* and *Pomona* sailed from points along the North Shore to Pier 18, North River.

During the middle years of the 19th century there was much activity amongst the various church groups of Staten Island and many houses of worship were erected.

Woodrow United Methodist Church, built 1842. SIHS.

The first Methodist Society was organized in May 1787, following the wide interest in Methodism which the several visits of Francis Asbury had inspired. He had first preached in 1771 at the home of Peter van Pelt in Woodrow and it was close by that the first Methodist church later stood, and in which, during his subsequent visits, Bishop Asbury preached. The present edifice was built in 1842. In 1845 another church building of much architectural charm, the Moravian at New Dorp, was consecrated, and this, together with the Castleton Hill Church and the Great Kills Moravian Church constitute one collegiate congregation of the United Brethren. On an early map of Staten Island during the Revolution there appears the designation "Gambold's Church" and this is the edifice, consecrated 1763, which antedated the present one at New Dorp, the Rev. Hector Gambold being its first minister.

From 1839 to 1849 St. Peter's was the only Roman Catholic Church on Staten Island and was an outgrowth of one of the congregations which had used as a place of worship an abandoned gun factory near Lafayette Avenue. There is little recorded concerning Catholic services during the early years, but there were during Governor Dongan's administration several Jesuit priests in New York and it is not unlikely that mass was held in the Governor's manor house on Staten Island. St.

Mary's in Rosebank was organized in 1852 and a frame building was used until 1858, when the present church was dedicated. In Richmondtown, on the morning of March 17, 1862, the cornerstone of St. Patrick's Church was laid. St. Clare's in Great Kills enjoys the distinction of being the first Catholic church in the United States to be built in the colonial or federal style of architecture.

St. Paul's Episcopal Church, organized in 1833, celebrated the consecration of its first edifice two years later; the present church dates from 1870. The year 1844 witnessed the dedication of St. John's Episcopal Church of Clifton, located opposite the present building, the cornerstone of which was laid 1869. St. Simon's, in Concord, began about 1854 as a mission of the Clifton organization. St. Luke's of Rossville was built 1843 and the edifice which first housed the congregation of Christ Church in New Brighton was built 1849. A year earlier St. Mary's, also Episcopal, was organized and the original structure, dedicated 1853, formed the nave of the building which was recently destroyed by fire, but since rebuilt.

In 1856 the First Presbyterian Church was organized and its chapel on Townsend Avenue, Clifton, dedicated. It is this congregation which at the present time worships in the church on Brownell Street, dedicated 1894. The first Presbyterian meeting house on Staten Island was still standing at Stony Brook, a location between New Dorp and Oakwood, during the early part of the last century and, it is likely, was standing as early as 1729, for it is recorded that Jacques Cortelyou bestowed in that year a small piece of land, upon which stood a public meeting house, to several elders and deacons of the Presbyterian Society. Calvary Presbyterian Church was organized in 1872 and the present building, dedicated 1894 replaced the original structure, which was burned 1892.

Governor Daniel D. Tompkins gave the Tompkinsville property upon which, in 1818, a Reformed Protestant Dutch Church was built, and of which the Rev. Peter J. Van Pelt was for a few years pastor. This Church in 1870 became the Reformed Church of Brighton Heights. In 1849 the Reformed Protestant Dutch Church was organized in the school house at Huguenot and two years later was built its house of worship. This was burned 1918. The present church building was dedicated 1924.

The Clove Baptist Church stood for many years on the north slope of Emerson Hill, at Concord, and the site is marked by a few gravestones. It was built 1809, although the organization took place 1765, subsequent to which date open air meetings or gatherings in various barns and houses were held.

Previous to the war between the States two of our now prominent German Protestant Churches were organized. The Evangelical Lutheran in Port Richmond, now St. John's, was incorporated in 1852, while 1857 saw the incorporation of the German Evangelical Lutheran Church in Stapleton. It is now known as Trinity Evangelical Lutheran and the present edifice was dedicated 1914. Of the Jewish faith, the Congregation B'nai Jeshurun became incorporated in 1888.

VII

The Civil War Years

WITH the outbreak of the Civil War the Island again found itself host to the military. Situated close to New York, and possessed of unlimited areas which could be utilized for the encampment and training of troops, and for their subsequent embarkation for the war front, it became the assembly point for regiments in process of organization. Many of these, awaiting the arrival of recruits necessary to bring their enlisted personnel up to authorized strength, were ferried from New York and nearby points and established in various camps. The old Quarantine area at Tompkinsville was the site for two of these, Camps Washington and Arthur. The Smith farm, at Old Town, became Camp Scott; the New Dorp area contained Camps Vanderbilt, Yates and Lafayette, while more than a half dozen other cantonments were scattered along the East and North shores. Most of the troops were from distant cities and towns, and, reading accounts of their behavior while in training, it is easy to understand how completely dislocated was the economic and social life of the community. It is indeed a sordid picture which is painted for us by the writers of the period.

During the initial phase of the struggle young men responded to the call for volunteers in satisfactory numbers, in some localities exceeding the prescribed quotas. However, following the first surge of enthusiasm, recruiting fell off, and despite the flag raisings, oratory, and promises of liberal bounties, it soon became apparent that a system of conscription would have to be formulated. Serious disorder ensued when the likelihood of a draft became certain. The following is from Bayles' History of Richmond County:

"From its proximity to New York City this county could not but feel every pulsation of popular emotion that disturbed the bosom of that city, and when the celebrated draft riots of July, 1863, filled it with the horrors of an inferno it is perhaps no more than a reasonable consequence that some kindred spirit should find expression here. On the island the public mind was in a state of high fermentation. Riot was in the air, and it would seem that men hardly knew what they did. For two years the public mind here had been almost constantly wrought up to fever heat, and now the prospect of a draft being made to fill the quota of four hundred men in this county under the recent call, but few of whom were already enlisted, made a strain upon the public nerve which it was in poor condition to bear with tranquility. For a moment the steady arm of patriotism seemed to falter, weakened as it had been by the drain upon it caused by the withdrawal of hundreds from the community to the field of war. Sober counsel wavered and the influence of men of means was weak, because of the obnoxious clause in the conscription act which promised to exempt all drafted men who should pay three hundred dollars. In this weak moment the baser elements of society gathered strength, and disorder attempted to block the wheels of organized government.

"In this critical moment the innocent colored population were among the first to receive the demoniacal thrusts of unchained hatred. In McKeon Street, Stapleton, a large number of this class resided, and there was located their African church. On Tuesday evening, July 14th, crowds began to gather and indications of trouble appeared that alarmed the people of this neighborhood with fears that an attack upon them and upon this church was about to be made. Rumors were circulated that a mob was about to burn the houses of the negros and their church, but the night passed without any such demonstration being made.

"About the same time a large crowd, variously estimated to number from fifty to two hundred persons, a large number of whom were boys, proceeded to the Tompkins Lyceum, in Van Duzer Street, and with the noisy demonstrations of a band of wild Indians, forced the outer door, and took all the muskets that were stored there in the drill-room of the Tompkins cadets. Another drill-room near Stapleton landing was similarly robbed of muskets. Different estimates placed the number of guns thus seized by this mob at from thirty to three hundred.

"The mob, gathering numerical strength as it went, reached the Vanderbilt landing railroad station at about midnight, where they set fire to a building used as a car house, and burned it to the ground. Two engine companies who came to the scene were forbidden to interfere, but they were permitted to direct their efforts toward saving the dwelling of Mrs. Corson, which stood near by, and in this they succeeded.

"The nucleus of another mob was formed on the same evening at Factoryville, which proceeded eastward, gathering strength as it proceeded, making night hideous with shouts of 'No Draft' and many other violent and threatening expressions, too odious to be repeated. At New Brighton they proceeded to the ice cream saloon of a colored man by the name of Green, who fortunately had been apprised of their coming, and had closed his place and fled. They then entered the drug store of Mr. Christie with such noisy demonstrations that the proprietor fled to the cellar for safety. . . .

"On the afternoon of the following day a mob, consisting of nearly fifty men, made an attack upon the houses of the negros living in McKeon Street, Stapleton. These were mostly small one-story houses. One after another the windows were broken in, the doors torn down and the furniture and materials inside broken up and thrown into the street. The inmates of these houses had fled to the woods on the previous evening, and this, no doubt, saved some of their lives. One house . . . was burned to the ground. A three-story brick house occupied by families in the upper stories and a grocery store below, was completely 'gutted,' the mob helping themselves to groceries as they were thrown into the street. In one of the houses a lame man had remained. He was dragged from his house and heartlessly beaten, and others were kicked and beaten as they were met on the highways. An attempt was made to burn the church . . . a colored coachman was attacked. . . .

"On the north side of the island . . . many families packed up their valuables and left their houses. . . . The negros fled, some to the woods, and some to the Jersey shore."

Following these manifestations of hostility to enforced service in the armed forces an effort was made by the county officials to assure the public that they were not unsympathetic with their problem, and promises were given, in a huge meeting at Clifton, that an effort would be made to test the constitutionality of the Conscription Act before the State courts, and, in the event that this body should find the Act constitutional, it was resolved that substitutes would be provided for all who were unable or unwilling to serve. It would cost the county three hundred dollars per man, but it was considered advisable in the interest of the public good to meet that expense.

The draft mechanism was set in motion late in August, 1863, and out of the twenty-two hundred eligible men in the

county there were drawn five hundred ninety-four, and these
notified to appear before the provost marshal at Jamaica, Long
Island. But the majority took advantage of the three hundred
dollar clause in the Conscription Act, while those who did not
do so either furnished substitutes or were exempt on the
grounds of physical disability or were aliens. One hundred
fifty simply did not bother to report. In October the President
issued another call for troops, and this was repeated the following March. This time the county Supervisors decided to let
out a contract for filling the quota of a hundred men and the
requisite number were raised, with two hundred dollars paid
to each recruit and one hundred fifty dollars to the contractor
who produced him. There was another call by the President
in July, and the Supervisors were again called upon to solve
the problem of furnishing men. Under this last call the quota
was five hundred forty-three, and the officials, from their recruiting office at Tompkinsville offered two hundred dollars
per man and a like amount to the broker who procured him.
Any citizen whose name had been drawn had but to pay six
hundred dollars to the Supervisors and everything would be
taken care of. This figure was soon raised to seven hundred
dollars, but even with this inducement the quota was, in September, short by one hundred eighty men, and the county,
understandably short of cash, was unable to contract for these.
But bonds were put up, and by this arrangement the quota was
filled.

Finally, in February 1865, the draft, which up until then
had been rendered more or less inoperative on Staten Island
by reason of the county's ability to furnish the necessary men,
summoned by name four hundred and forty-six individuals.
But these were still entitled to exemption by the expedient of
hiring others to serve in their places. And, with the war's end

in sight, even this inconvenience was spared them. The coming of peace found the county heavily in debt, the Supervisors nervous wrecks, and its mercantile activities at a low ebb. But more than two thousand Staten Islanders had helped gain the victory upon the field of battle.

It was during the restless years of the war that George William Curtis's influence as a writer and orator began to be felt. Born in Rhode Island in 1824, he came to the Island in 1856, immediately assuming a profound interest in its affairs. A Republican and an abolitionist, he was the principal speaker at every political meeting in the campaign of 1860, and later, when hostilities commenced, his remarkable eloquence persuaded many a luke-warm individual to enlist. He was a singularly handsome person, cultured, brilliant and broadhearted, one of our most beloved citizens.

PARSONS & ATWATER DEL. N.Y.   Entered according to Act of Congress AD 1869 by Currier & Ives in the Clerks Office of the District Court of the United States for the Southern District of N.Y.   Reprinted from LITH. BY CURRIER & IVES.

THE NEW YORK YACHT CLUB REGATTA.

THE START FROM THE STAKE BOAT IN THE NARROWS,

VIII

The Problems of Expansion

IN that period of Staten Island's development which followed the Civil War the thought uppermost in the minds of those men who believed in a bright and prosperous future for New York's southernmost county was improvement. Lying at the threshold of one of the great cities of the world, its rolling hills enchanting all who gazed upon them, it was bound to prove tremendously attractive to home seekers in ever increasing numbers; it was also inevitable that its waterfront would tempt many who sensed advantages to those industries which could be located close to a fine seaport. During the middle years of the 19th century most Americans were briskly engaged in devising means of obtaining wealth, for opportunities for success were plentiful as the fruit on Peter Kalm's cherry trees. Events were on the move; everyone desired to better his lot.

Staten Islanders were just as practical as the rest of the nation and just as willing to do business. One thing they possessed was land, and this they offered to the highest bidders by the lot, acre, and plot. But despite the artfully phrased advertisements and pamphlets there was a scarcity of customers for property upon "this most 'Beautiful Isle of the Sea' with its sea-girt shores, decked with costly villas and thrifty villages, its romantic rides, its picturesque hills of smiling green crowned with grand old forests, its cool, shaded valleys, and its landscape diversified everywhere with palatial villas, rural homes and cottages nestling amid the roses; art emulating nature in everything calculated to charm the taste and delight the imagination." Whatever it was which was to blame for the

"The New York Yacht Club Regatta, The Start from the Stake Boat in the Narrows." Currier & Ives, 1869. SIHS.

paucity of land sales, it certainly could not have been the ad-writer.

The local gain in population for the five years, 1865-1870, was far below that of towns in Westchester and Long Island. So patent was this disparity that the Legislature in 1870 appointed a commission to make an investigation, then submit a report and a plan for necessary improvements on the Island, as well as suggestions for improving the means of communication between it and adjacent territory, especially New York. Nine months later the gentlemen detailed to this work had diagnosed the cause of the Island's backwardness as malaria and poor ferry service. Regarding the former, they believed that its prevalence and severity were greatly exaggerated, but recommended an elaborate system of drainage, averring that "if Staten Island can be freed from malaria, it will be a comparatively easy matter to make it the healthiest, and at the same time the most convenient and most beautiful suburb of New York." Their comment concerning the ferry service amounted to unvarnished condemnation. "The boats have most uncomfortable seats, are badly ventilated, and at night badly lighted. Being, also, short-handed, or with inadequate organization of service for their duty, passengers suffer from disorder and nuisances which might easily be prevented. These little matters make all the difference between misery and comfort to many, especially many women. The landing places and houses are in every way the reverse of attractive and convenient."

It was not long after this that the ferryboat *Westfield*, lying in a slip at the foot of Whitehall Street with four hundred passengers aboard, blew up as a result of a boiler explosion. Nearly a hundred lives were lost, while twice that number were seriously injured. This was the end of the ferry company, whose finances failed to survive the shock, and a new company took over its affairs. The *Westfield* was rebuilt and, together with other boats of the line, continued to ply between New York and the East Shore, while a disgruntled public continued to complain concerning the wretched service. There was a line of ferryboats connecting New York and Port Richmond, with the first company beginning operations in 1823, and travel on both routes must have been quite an adventure, what with the rival skippers racing up or down the bay, and their boats running upon the reefs or becoming frozen in the ice. Reading the more or less confused account of the mishaps, financial and otherwise, which befell the ferries one can readily understand why Staten Island's development was retarded. However, there was considerable improvement in the service after the Rapid Transit Railroad Company and the Baltimore and Ohio began to operate the Whitehall Street to Staten Island line. In 1905 it became the Municipal Ferry, and today a fleet of fast boats is in use, daily carrying thousands of commuters to business in Manhattan, and enjoying the reputation of offering the best five-cent water trip in the world.

Stages had carried Staten Islanders over the main roads since before the Revolution, and during the mid-nineteenth century there seem to have been many lines connecting the inland villages and the ferries. In 1869 Samuel Sneden ran stages between Castleton Corners and Vanderbilt Landing; there were four trips a day by Taylor's stages between New Dorp and Green Ridge via Richmondtown; one Thomas Dubois operated between Huguenot and Rossville; while Thompson's stage travelled over the roads which connected Port Richmond and Richmondtown.

Horse drawn rail cars first ran in 1863 from Tompkinsville, by way of Jersey Street, to Port Richmond. Later this line was extended to Holland Hook, where the present ferry to Elizabeth is located. A connecting line ran along Bay Street from Tompkinsville to Fort Wadsworth. By 1885 horse cars left the foot of Broadway and travelled over that and adjacent thoroughfares to the brewery above Castleton Corners. Still another line had one terminus at the park in Stapleton and the other in Concord, and when roads were covered with snow sleighs were utilized, their floors heaped with straw so that the customers' feet would not freeze.

An attempt was made as early as 1836 to start the operation of a steam railway between the East Shore and Tottenville, and a corporation was formed. However, since two years elapsed with nothing accomplished in the way of physical achievement the charter became void. But in 1851 a new company organized and after numerous delays there was a track laid part of the way to the south end of the Island. In March, 1860, the first locomotive, the *Albert Journeay,* a wood burner, made its debut, and according to the local press of the period, astonished the citizenry. Everyone rushed to see the locomotive. One old man, who cackled that he had never seen one of the contraptions, declared that he had walked five miles from his place of habitation close to Skunk's Misery. When it came snorting along the rails he jumped a foot or so, exclaimed "I swow!" then clapped his jaws (presumably edentulous) together and remained dumb the rest of the day.

Soon another engine, the *Edward Banker,* made its appearance, and by June 2 the line was open to Tottenville. There were celebrations, with dinners and speeches, and everyone vowed that this was the enterprise destined to "give an impetus to the growth of the Island beyond the most sanguine expectations." But the company found itself in difficulties because of the lack of sufficient capital and went into bankruptcy. Mr.

W. H. Vanderbilt, of New Dorp, was appointed receiver, and under his management the trains continued to function.

There has been a conscious effort throughout this short history to avoid introducing names of Prominent Citizens. These will be found in the larger works relating to the Island's story, numerous as raisins in a plum pudding, and, since local histories are customarily issued on a subscription basis, are especially profuse in those sections chronologically synchronous with the work's publication. The name of Erastus Wiman is, however, one which may not be omitted. He was born in 1834 near Toronto, Canada, and, following some years as a journalist, came to New York as manager of the commercial agency of R. G. Dun & Co. Shortly after this he came to Staten Island and made his home close to the shore at Great Kills. Keen of mind, forceful and energetic, he went to work on the problem of improving the Island's system of transportation, and under the stimulating influence of his leadership much was accomplished.

The Staten Island Rapid Transit Railroad Company, organized in 1880, acquired the East Shore-New York ferries. Soon thereafter rail service along the north shore from St. George to Elm Park, and along the east shore from St. George to South Beach was an accomplished fact, both starting in 1886. The old line previously in operation from St. George to Tottenville had in the meanwhile been leased to the company. Having what he considered an adequate system of rail and water transportation, Mr. Wiman set about the task of attracting customers for his trains and boats. He had a bit of the Billy Rose flair for doing things in a big way, and spent thirty-five thousand dollars in the erection at St. George of a three story Casino. The attractions here were illuminated fountains and a sixty piece band in the evenings, while during the afternoons there were baseball and lacrosse. Purcell of Manhattan had the restaurant concession, and five thousand persons could be accommodated upon the Casino's two galleries, from which a panoramic view of the harbor was obtained. The fountains are richly described in the advertisement of the S. I. Amusement Company, in 1886: "At the further end of the park the wonderful fountains, illuminated by electric light, with which Sir Francis Bolton, the electrician, delighted London, will throw their many hued jets a hundred feet in air . . . imagine a big square pond with a great column of water shooting upward from its centre, and breaking into a cloud of spray away up in the air and around this central column a circle of minor jets, too numerous for counting, crossing each other at such angles and in such number that one seems to be looking at a vast aqueous birdcage surmounted and encircled by mist clouds —and all this illuminated from the mysterious subterranean chamber by powerful electric lights, shining through lenses of all colors, changed with kaleidoscopic rapidity."

This proved quite a sensation; thousands from Manhattan and New Jersey and hundreds from points upon the Island came to gape at the spectacle much as we, not long ago, gaped at the same sort of thing in the New York World's Fair. But attendance soon dropped; the power station with its two engine-driven generators which had delivered energy for this watery exhibition was purchased by the Edison Electric Illuminating Company, about to embark upon a village lighting project. So Wiman tried a girl show the following year, with Kiralfy Brothers—remembered by some of us for their "Carnival of Venice" at Happyland, South Beach, in 1906—furnishing the talent and scenic effects. "The Fall of Babylon" was their first attraction, in 1887, and they touched up the settings the following year, added a few more girls and a herd of elephants, putting it on as "The Fall of Rome."

New Yorkers who had no liking for this opulent type of entertainment were able to enjoy something a trifle less cloying at Erastina, a location on the railroad beyond Port Richmond which had been named for Wiman. This was Buffalo Bill's Wild West Show, and twelve thousand persons could be accommodated in the grandstand to view the exhibitions of horsemanship, lariat throwing and rifle marksmanship. Folks came from far and near to see the show. Even the late Clarence Day, as part of his youthful education, was taken, following a hearty lunch at Delmonico's to see it by his imperious papa, little dreaming that years later "Life with Father" would establish a record for theatrical attendance.

Mr. Wiman died in his seventieth year, with little to show for his devotion to the cause of Staten Island's civic and commercial advancement. It was said of him, in a contemporary editorial, that "he planted well and others will reap the harvest. Some of the improvements of Staten Island for which he labored so incessantly are at hand, and when they are an established fact due honor should be given Mr. Wiman for any part he may have had in their inception."

Note: Erastus Wiman's permanent home was on St. Marks Place, in the house that was for years occupied by the Staten Island Club, later by the Elks' Club.

IX

Political Synthesis

BY 1896 Staten Island's population had topped sixty thousand and could boast of fifty-four miles of macadam and Telford roads, fifty-three churches of eight denominations, fifteen benevolent institutions, twenty-nine public and eleven private and parochial schools, forty-one social, scientific and benevolent societies, nine banks and building loan associations, three private water companies, twenty post offices, thirty-five volunteer fire companies, sixty-six policemen, twelve newspapers, twenty-eight industries employing fifty or more men, two small electric companies, one gas company, one telephone company. As a community it had done well, and everyone entertained high hopes for a continuance of its prosperity and advancement when it became part of the City of New York, for the consolidation bill had been passed in the Senate.

A charter was drafted and submitted to the Legislature in February 1897 and in the following November election George Cromwell was chosen first president of the Borough of Richmond. As Richmond County the Island continued to be represented by county officials at Albany. The offices of county treasurer and supervisors were eliminated, however, since taxes were collected and expenses paid by the city, while village presidents, clerks and trustees were legislated out of office. Villages, as such, ceased to exist but the names of a few still persist, and the reader will find these included in the list to be found in the appendix.*

It was during the first year of Mr. Cromwell's incumbency that the Spanish-American War began. The battleship *Maine,*

Borough President George Cromwell speaking at Borough Hall dedication, May 21, 1904. SIHS.

* See page 107.

familiar to Staten Islanders who had many times seen it at its anchorage off Tompkinsville, was destroyed in Havana harbor February 15, 1898, and war was declared April 21. Many Staten Islanders enlisted in the Volunteers and in the State regiments, but the war produced few casualties. Most of the local excitement occasioned by the conflict occurred when, just previous to the outbreak of hostilities, the Spanish cruiser *Viscaya,* making a "friendly" call, dropped anchor at the identical spot where the *Maine* had once peacefully floated, producing in East Shore residents a state of mind half indignation and half fear of being blown to bits. However, the ship steamed away before the declaration of war and joined Cevera's fleet at Santiago, where, during the historic battle, it was destroyed along with the Admiral's other cruisers. At the termination of the war the *Maine* as well as several of the enemy's ships was salvaged by the Merritt Chapman Company of Stapleton, and in no other town in the country was the juvenile population subsequently so well-supplied with war materiel and nautical equipment, all of it showing evidence of having been submerged in salt water, yet doubly desirable because of it.

During the first four years following consolidation considerable work was done on the Island's roads, and Mr. Cromwell undertook the task of obtaining certain necessary improvements such as a building for the borough administrative offices, a centrally located high school, a fire alarm system, better water supply, and an amelioration of the transportation difficulties, all of which were effected within the space of a few years. The city took over the ferry in 1905 and five large modern boats which had been built were placed in service. Curtis High School, named in honor of George William Curtis, had been opened a year previous, while 1906 saw the dedication of the new Borough Hall. The Island had embarked upon a new, fresh phase of prosperous and satisfactory development.

This modest work can not, for obvious reasons, describe in detail the events of Richmond Borough's early years. Many industrial plants began operation. Carnegie libraries were opened, branches were established by Manhattan banking concerns. .The great retaining wall was built at St. George.

Our Island has been visited by blizzards, hurricanes, and chestnut blight. We have suffered from destructive fires, the New Jersey smoke nuisance, Japanese beetles and strikes. We enjoy Christmas trees in our public squares during the Yuletide, and in those same recreational areas, where a generation ago the town's small fry slid into first base, one now finds comfort stations of various designs. Golfers come from other boroughs to play upon our splendid links. We have had county fairs, beach carnivals, drinking fountains for horses, baby parades, tree plantings and trackless trolleys. The Island is proud of its colleges, its large zoo and two fine museums. Of the latter, the Staten Island Institute of Arts and Sciences occupies two buildings at St. George; the Staten Island Historical Society pursues its activities in Richmondtown, the former county seat, housing its collections in the old County Clerk's office and in the century old white-pillared court house opposite. It is this latter organization which has embarked upon the project of Richmondtown's restoration. Many citizens enjoy membership in the Rotary, Kiwanis, and Lions Clubs, while some of these, along with others, play in the Staten Island Symphony Society's fine orchestra. Three immense bridges facilitate travel to and from New Jersey, and another, which will be the world's largest, is being planned to span the Narrows. The Island is an increasingly busy place with its factories, shipyards, supermarkets, and the great Foreign Trade Zone Number One on the East Shore.

However, much that is rural remains. In Richmondtown one may still wander amongst the old gravestones in St. Andrew's churchyard, and, in the Voorlezer's House nearby, contemplate a late 17th century schoolroom. The road along the salt meadows could not have looked much different then than now, and wild duck, red-winged blackbirds, and muskrat still haunt the winding waterways of the Fresh Kills.

We are indeed fortunate in having these things about us; they are good for our minds and for our souls, and it is hoped that state and municipal acquisition of large unimproved areas will increase before it is too late, to the end that our descendants may be assured an escape from metropolitan hubbub to sylvan peace without being obliged to journey a hundred miles from home. The late William T. Davis, historian, entomologist, and naturalist loved Staten Island and during his long and busy lifetime became more familiar with its topography, its flora and fauna, than perhaps any other man. He loved to go alone afield, and could see in the outdoors a hundred times more than could an ordinary individual. He was not much of a traveller, as we understand the term, yet, save during those times when he was writing, he was seldom indoors. He wrote a book* which is a delight to read not once, but many times, and an excerpt from it provides a gracious close to this brief story of our Island:

"It is often well to select some circumscribed piece of mother earth, and watch it particularly throughout the year, comparing it with the other fields to which occasional journeys are made. The rhythm of the warmer months is broken by scatter-

Old Mill Road, Richmond with Church of St. Andrew in distance, 1895. SIHS.

* William T. Davis, *Days Afield on Staten Island*, (N. Y. 1937).

ing our observation too wide. There is a cadence of the year; one continuous song changing gradually and almost imperceptibly, and of which each musical creature sings in turn his part. The first outburst of melody of the song-sparrow, the black birds in the swamp, the crickets, the katydids, the *z-ing* of the harvest flies, and the late fall notes of the birds going southwards; these and many more, all come as signs of the seasons, and mark for each patch of mother earth the progress of the year. They make a beautiful and pathetic march, and are best seen and most forcibly impressed by looking steadily at the same acres. If we stand with open eyes, there is no pageant so varied as the march of the warmer days. But the rapid change that characterizes Summer is gone in Winter. There may be snow or there may be none, but we have generally to look close to note that a few more dead leaves have blown off an oak on the hillside, or that the blackhaw berries are a little more shrivelled than they were a month ago. When the ban of Boreas is o'er the land, and the leaves huddle together in the depressions in the woods, as if they would keep one another warm, and the snow lies on the earth, then a view of one field, of one hillside, is so similar to the view a month hence that one falls back on the calendar for the want of any change betokening the march of time out of doors.

"Nature does indeed will us strange fortunes, but generally she is tolerably kind, and if we do not try to visit the North Pole, or spend a Summer in the Sahara, we may live along without any break in our mutual, friendly relations. We may go musing calmly in the meadows, in the woodland, and along the country lanes, and hark to those inward murmurings of fancy that cause a strange array of natural and human transactions to move in turn over old Staten Island, that seems to sleep so peacefully today beneath the Autumn sun. The patroons and their Bouweries, the Peach War, the British troops quartered on the Island, and the domestic scenes in the Dutch and Hugenot families, wear to us a garment of quiet and pleasing interest, though its seams chafed harshly enough many of those who wore it of old. No doubt the present is quite as unquiet and wrangling as many a bygone year, but over the past there always rests a halo, and time, like a kind critic, idealizes for us the jumbled maze, and only gives forth a poetic tincture of the whole."

Saint George, ca. 1909. New York Public Library, left; Brighton Heights Reformed Church, center; and Borough Hall, right. SIHS.

Cutting ice, Silver Lake. Photograph by Charles T. Whitehorn, 1905. SIHS.

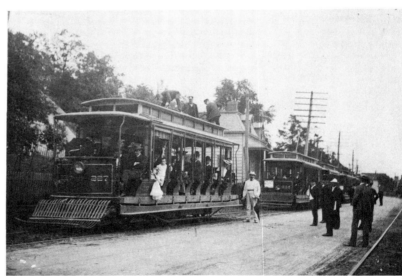

Midland trolley cars at fairgrounds, Dongan Hills. 1905. SIHS.

BIBLIOGRAPHY

AKERLY, SAMUEL, M. D., *Agriculture of Staten Island.* (Trans. N. Y. State Agl. Soc., II, 188-214, 1842. Supplement, Assembly, No. 100, 1843.)

ANTHON, JOHN, and his son CHARLES E., *Anthon's Notes,* pub. by the S. I. Inst. of Arts and Sciences.

BAYLES, RICHARD M., *History of Richmond County.* New York, 1887.

BEAUCHAMP, WILLIAM M., *Aboriginal Occupation of New York,* Bull. No. 32, N. Y. State Mus., 1900.
    A History of the New York Iroquois. Albany, 1905.

BOLTON, R. P., *The Old Fort and Camp Site at Richmond.* (N. Y. Hist. Soc. Quar. Bull. III, 82-88, Oct., 1919.)

BRODHEAD, J. R., *History of the State of New York.* New York, 1853-71.

CLUTE, JOHN J., *Annals of Staten Island from its Discovery to the Present Time.* New York, 1877.

DAVIS, WILLIAM T., *Days Afield on Staten Island.* Staten Island, 1892.
    Staten Island Names, Ye Olde Names and Nicknames, with map by C. W. Leng. (Proc. Nat. Sci. Assn., S. I., 1896, and Supplement, 1903.)
    The Conference or Billopp House. Staten Island, 1926.
    The Church of St. Andrew. (With C. W. Leng and R. W. Vosburgh.) Staten Island, 1925.
    Staten Island and Its People New York, 1930.
    The North Shore S. I., 1925

DELAVAN, EDWARD C., JR., *Indian Deed of Staten Island to Governor Lovelace, 1670.* (Proc. Nat. Sci. Assn. of S. I., II, p. 79, May 9, 1891.)
    The First English Grants of Land Upon Staten Island. (Idem, VI, 28-29, 31-32, May 8 and June 12, 1897.)
    Col. Francis Lovelace and His Plantation on Staten Island. (Idem, VII, 47-79, Mar. 10, 1900; and VIII, p. 62, April 11, 1903.)

DE VRIES, DAVID PIETERSZ, *Korte Historiael ende Journaels, 1655,* translated in Coll. N. Y. Hist. Soc. 1841.

Documents Relating to Colonial History, 15 vols.

Documentary History of New York, 4 vols.

Ecclesiastic Records, State of New York, Albany, 1901-02.

FISKE, JOHN, *The Dutch and Quaker Colonies in America.*

FLICK, ALEXANDER C., *The American Revolution in New York.* Albany, 1926.

GUERNSEY, R. S., *New York City During War of 1812.* N. Y., 1889.

HAMPTON, VERNON B., *Staten Island's Claim to Fame.* Staten Island, 1925.

HINE, CHARLES GILBERT, *Ye Old Perine House.* N. Y., 1915.
    History-Story-Legend-Old King's Highway. N. Y., 1916.
    Howard Avenue & Serpentine Road N. Y., 1914.
    The North Shore S. I., 1925

HOLLICK, DR. FREDERICK, *The Old Quarantine, Its Destruction, etc.* (Proc. Nat. Sci. Assn. S. I., Vol. III, pp. 64-67, Oct. 1893.)

HUBBELL, ARTHUR Y., *Prominent Men of Staten Island.* S. I., 1893.

JAMESON, DR. J. FRANKLIN, *Narratives of New Netherland, 1609-64.* Trans. of original narratives of Hudson's voyages, etc. N. Y., 1909.

KALM, PETER, *Travels into North America.* Tr. by J. R. Foster. London, 1772.

LAMB, MARTHA J., and HARRISON, MRS. BURTON, *History of the City of New York.* 3 vols. N. Y., 1877.

LENG, CHARLES W., *Ecclesiastical History of Staten Island in the 17th Century.* (Proc. S. I. Inst. Arts and Sciences, II, 113-25, May, 1923.)
    Staten Island and Its People New York, 1930

MELYN, CORNELIUS, *Melyn Papers.* Coll. N. Y. Hist. Soc. 1913.

MILLER, REV. JOHN, *New York Considered and Improved, London, 1695.* With Introduction and Notes by Victor Hugo Paltsits. Cleveland, 1903.

MOORE, FRANK, *Diary of the American Revolution.* N. Y., 1863.

MORRIS, IRA K., *Memorial History of Staten Island.* 2 vols. N. Y., 1898-00.

New York Genealogical and Biographical Record.

New York Historical Society Collections.

Reports of President, Borough of Richmond.

Proceedings of the S. I. Institute of Arts & Sciences.

SINGLETON, ESTHER, *Social New York Under the Georges.* N. Y., 1902.

SMITH, WILLIAM, *History of the Province of New York from the First Discovery to the Year 1732.*

Staten Island Historian, quarterly publication of the S. I. Historical Society.

STILLWELL, DR. JOHN E., *Historical and Genealogical Miscellany,* 4 vols. 1903-16.

STUART, JAMES, *Three Years in North America.* 1833.

TREVELYN, SIR GEORGE OTTO, *The American Revolution.* 3 vols. N. Y., 1908.

VOSBURGH, ROYDON W., *The Settlement of New Netherland, 1624-26.* (N. Y. Gen. and Biog. Records. L. V. 3-15, 1924.)

Sailors' Snug Harbor, New Brighton, begun 1831. Photograph by E. T. Clegg, ca. 1900. SIHS.

OLD PLACE NAMES

Compiled from *Staten Island Names, Ye Olde Names and Nicknames* by William T. Davis.

ANNADALE—A station on the Staten Island Railroad, named in honor of Mrs. Anna S. Seguine, about 1860.

ARDEN, WOODS OF—A large tract of woodland so named by Erastus Wiman about 1886.

ARLINGTON—A station on the Staten Island Rapid Transit Railroad near Mariners' Harbor, so named about 1886.

ARROCHAR—A settlement near Fort Wadsworth, started by W. W. MacFarland about 1880 and named from his recollections of the hills of Arrochar at the northern end of Loch Lomond, Scotland.

BLOOMFIELD—A small settlement in the sandy region south of Old Place, the name appearing on the 1874 Beer's Atlas.

BULL'S HEAD—At the corner of Richmond Avenue and the Turnpike, now the Victory Boulevard. The locality took its name from a tavern which formerly stood at the junction of these two highways.

BUTCHERVILLE—On the Watchogue or Butcherville Road, between the Willowbrook Road and Richmond Avenue. It is mentioned in a tax sale, December, 1890, but is of much more ancient origin.

CHELSEA—A small village on the western side of the Island, fronting on the Arthur Kill, and during the Revolution called Pralltown.

CLIFTON—An east shore village, laid out in 1837 and later included in the incorporated village of Edgewater. According to the New York State Manual it was called Bay View Post Office from 1858 to 1863.

CLOVENA—An area in the Clove Valley near Richmond Turnpike, now Victory Boulevard, was known by this name, probably bestowed upon it by a land development company.

CONCORD—Named, about 1845, by Thoreau and the Emersons. It had been previously known as Dutch Farms.

CASTLETON FOUR CORNERS—At the junction of Manor Road and the Victory Boulevard. The post office bearing this name is first so mentioned in 1872; on maps of 1850, 1859, and 1860 it is called Centerville.

CEDAR GROVE—This is shown on maps of 1850, 1860, and 1872.

CHARLESTON—See Kreischerville.

COURT HOUSE—Early name for the railroad station now called Oakwood Heights. It was still earlier called Club House.

CUCKOLDSTOWN—A corruption of Cocclestown, early name for Richmondtown, antedating the Revolution.

DONGAN HILLS—This includes the former Garretson's area and part of Old Town.

DOVER—The name given to a settlement near the present Arrochar by English settlers.

EDGEWATER—This is the name under which the east shore village was incorporated in 1866.

EGBERTVILLE—This is the area at the junction of Richmond Road and Rockland Avenue. It was called Morgan's Corner in 1838 and has been at various times known as Tipperary Corners, New Dublin, and Young Ireland.

ELM PARK—Called Jacksonville in 1829 and Lowville in 1849, it was the first dock on the north shore west of Port Richmond during the period when the North Shore Ferry was in operation.

ELTINGVILLE—Named for the Elting family. Until 1873 the post office for this vicinity was South Side; it then became Sea Side.

EMERSON HILL—This lies south of the Clove. Judge William Emerson came there to live in 1843.

ERASTINA—A railroad station named for Erastus Wiman and built at the time of Buffalo Bill's Wild West Show in 1886.

ELLIOTTVILLE—An old name for Livingston, named for Dr. Samuel MacKenzie Elliott.

ELM TREE—There was a huge tree standing at the foot of New Dorp Lane which was, according to Conner and Sprong's Map of 1797, "a mark for vessels leaving and going from New York to Amboy, Middletown and Brunswick." The present Elm Tree Light has taken its place.

FORT WADSWORTH—A name applied to the vicinity adjacent to the fortifications at the Narrows. Names previously applied have been Signal Hill, Flagstaff, The Telegraph, Lookout, as on Bew's Map of 1781, Conner and Sprong's of 1979, and Smith's of 1836, all in reference to its use as a point for signaling by semaphore before the days of electric telegraphy. On Blood's map of 1845 the names of the forts appear as Fort Richmond and Fort Tompkins. Beers' Atlas of 1874 records the defenses as Forts Tompkins and Wadsworth.

FOX HILL—According to W. T. Davis, this name first appears in the Report of the Staten Island Improvement Commission, 1871. During the nineties it was frequently referred to as Clifton Park.

FACTORYVILLE—This is first shown on a map filed by N. Barrett in 1836 and subsequently appears on maps of 1850, 1859, and 1860. Its post office was known as North Shore but was changed to West New Brighton in 1871.

GARRETSON'S—So called because of the Garretson farm. The Dongan Hills railroad station was formerly called Garretson's.

GRANT CITY—John C. Thompson commenced this development subsequent to the Civil War.

GRASMERE—This is a residential section south of the vicinity known as Fox Hills, and dates from about 1886.

GREAT KILLS—A rapidly growing community on the south shore, this was formerly called Gifford's. It was a mecca for fishermen and noted for the seafood served in its hotels.

GREEN RIDGE—This is a mile west of Richmondtown on the Arthur Kill Road, a locality now noted for its road stands. It is the site of the French Church, which was the place of worship for the many Huguenot families who settled there. It has been called Kleine Kill by the Dutch, Fresh Kill by the Colonial English, and has also been known as Marshland. Marshland Post Office is mentioned in the New York State Manual for 1874; in 1876 Green Ridge had taken its place. The picturesque ruins of the Benham mansion are here.

GIFFORDS—See Great Kills.

GRYMES' HILL—Overlooking the east short villages and the upper and lower bays, this was developed in 1830 by Major George Howard, for whom Howard Avenue is named. Madame Grymes came here to live in 1836. The story of this noted locality is told by Charles Gilbert Hine in his *History and Legend of Howard Avenue and Serpentine Road, Grymes' Hill, N. Y. 1914.*

GRANITEVILLE—In 1830 this was known as Fayetteville, but on maps of 1850 and later the names Granite Village and Graniteville appear, these originating with the quarries which were being worked.

HOLLAND HOOK—An old name for the northwestern corner of the Island and often erroneously called Howland Hook or Hollin's Hook. The origin of the name has been traced to Henry Holland, member of a wealthy New York family, who presented a silver alms basin to St. Andrew's Church, represented Staten Island in the Colonial Assembly, and owned a north shore estate called "Morning Star", as shown on a handbill offering the property for sale. J. J. Clute traces the name to a one-time preponderance of Dutch settlers in this region.

HUGUENOT—The name of a station on the railroad and, during the middle nineteenth century, known as Bloomingview.

KREISCHERVILLE—The locality, once known as Androvetteville or Andro-vettetown, is described in a local newspaper of 1856 as beautifully located near the water and containing "a mine of wealth both as regards purity of clay and pretty ladies." Balthasar Kreischer started the manufacture of firebrick here in 1854. Today the locality is probably more universally known as Charlston, which is the name of the post office.

LINDEN PARK—Between Old Town Road and Dongan Hills, this area is shown on a map filed in 1870 and on Dripps' map of 1872.

LINOLEUMVILLE—Named after a factory once located here. It was formerly part of Long Neck Village (Walling's Map of 1859). Long Neck Post Office was discontinued in 1866. An early name is New Blazing Star, as shown on 1793 and 1797 maps.

LIVINGSTON—This name, dating from 1886, was given to the locality previously known as Elliottville. The residence of the Livingston family became the railroad station. South Elliottville was the corner of Bard and Forest Avenues and Tangle-Wood was a tangled growth of catbrier and scrub on the westerly side of Bard Avenue where it crosses Castleton Avenue.

LAKE'S ISLAND—An island in the Arthur Kill, mentioned by Thoreau in 1843, and the scene of lively goings-on in 1916, when the operation of a garbage disposal plant at this point occasioned far more manifestations of displeasure on the part of the population than do the disposal projects now being carried out.

MANOR OF BENTLEY—Captain Christopher Billopp's grant of land at the southern tip of the Island.

MANOR OF CASSILTOWNE—Castle Town, later corrupted to Castleton, was land granted to John Palmer and subsequently conveyed to Governor Dongan. It was on the north shore and named after Dongan's home in County Kildare, Ireland.

MARINERS' HARBOR—This was a prosperous community while the oyster trade flourished during the years previous to consolidation. The affluence of those engaged in the business was reflected in the fine houses—Captains' Row—which faced the water. A few of these, interesting examples of classic revival architecture, still stand.

NARROWS—Sometimes used to designate the land adjoining the water passage between Fort Wadsworth and Fort Hamilton.

NEW BRIGHTON—First shown on a map in 1834. An extensive area which included Brighton or Hamilton Park, between Franklin and York Avenues; Jackson Park, at the corner of Franklin and Third Street; Tuxedo, at the end of Brighton Avenue; Dutch Block, a row of houses on the west side of Jersey Street a short distance from Richmond Terrace. The Goose Patch was an open field between Westervelt Avenue and Jersey Street, now traversed by Crescent Avenue.

NEW DORP—The original New Dorp was located at the foot of New Dorp Lane near the shore.

NORTH SIDE—The post office name for West New Brighton until 1871.

OAKWOOD HEIGHTS—See Court House.

OLD PLACE—On what was once called Tunissen's Neck, this has been nicknamed Skunk Town. Its eastern portion was known as Summerville.

OUDE DORP or OLD TOWN—The ancient town at South Beach where in 1679 the travelers Dankers and Sluyter found seven houses, of which only three were inhabited.

QUARANTINE—The present station is in Rosebank. The Quarantine was from 1799 to 1858 at Tompkinsville.

PRICE'S ISLAND—Name given to a hummock of land in the salt meadow south of Travis. Elias Price was a prominent resident on Long Neck circa 1830.

PRINCE'S BAY—The name for this territory on the south shore is of pre-revolutionary origin and various appelations have been applied to portions of it. Lemon Creek post office appears in the New York State Manual for 1859, replaced by Prince's Bay in 1861 and Prince Bay in recent years. The railroad has two stations, one at Prince's Bay and one at Pleasant Plains. The latter locality has been called The Plains, also Eeltown. A low, wet place along Sandy Brook between Pleasant Plains and Prince's Bay was in 1857 known as Skunk's Misery.

PORT RICHMOND—The Rev. James Brownlee was responsible for this name. The area was known as Burial Place at about the end of the seventeenth century and during the Revolution was called Decker's Ferry. At the time of consolidation Port Richmond was known as the Model Village, its special pride having been its neatly kept streets.

PROHIBITION PARK—The development now known as Westerleigh started as Prohibition Park in 1889. The sale of beer and liquor was prohibited within its boundaries. Many fine houses were built and it became known as an unusually progressive community. An immense auditorium, in which were given lectures and concerts, was an attraction. A huge stone fountain stood beside this structure, electrically lighted and pouring out the only liquid which enjoyed the sponsorship of the Park Association.

RICHMOND—The earliest known mention of Richmond as a village was in 1700 under the name of "Coccles Town." This name, often written "Cuckoldstown," disappeared during the Revolution and the name "Richmond Town," which had been used as early as 1728, became the accepted term. The origin of the word "Coccles

Town" might be found in the abundance of oyster and clam shells commonly called "coccle" shells in early days which were found in the waters of the Fresh Kills near Richmond.

By 1730, Richmond was a thriving village and the center of the County of Richmond. A court house, a jail, at least one tavern, ten or twelve houses, and the Church of St. Andrew made up the little village.

During the Revolution, Richmond Town was occupied by the British troops. Many of the buildings were utilized as quarters while a fort and huts were constructed on Richmond Hill, above the village. Several skirmishes took place in and near Richmond, and when finally the soldiers departed they left the Court House and the Dutch Church in ashes.

The change from Colonial to Federal government, in 1783, took place smoothly and found the little village quietly resuming its former activity.

The next eighty years saw many changes take place, mostly brought about by the growth of the Island. A new Court House was erected in 1794 and replaced in 1836-1837, a County Clerks and Surrogates office followed in 1848, and a jail in 1860. Richmond was the political and at times the social center of the Island.

The period from 1860 to 1898 was one of little change in the history of Richmond. In 1898, Staten Island became part of the Greater City of New York. Many county positions were eliminated and the value of Richmond as a county center decreased. In 1920 the last of the public offices were removed to St. George, a more convenient location, and with the old county buildings abandoned Richmond became a strictly residential village.

In 1932 the old Court House, and in 1935 the old County Clerks office, which were in need of repair, were restored by the Government, and the latter building turned over to the Historical Society for a Museum.

With the preservation of these buildings and others planned, Richmond entered a new and important period in its history as the Historical center of Staten Island.

Many of the old family names connected with early Richmond are as follows, Tilyer, Fitchet, Dye, Coone, Rezeau, Swain, Prall, Wood, Van Pelt, Frost, Crocheron, Moore, Marsh, Barton, Betts, Conner.

RICHMOND VALLEY—A railroad station at a point which has become the northern part of Tottenville.

ROSEBANK—This name was selected for a post office and a railroad station but has since been applied to the general vicinity.

ROSSVILLE—Named about 1837 in honor of Colonel William E. Ross, it was previously known as Old Blazing Star, after a tavern of that name. There was a ferry to New Jersey, and in 1886 it was described as "one of the important villages in the Town of Westfield" where "the boat plying between New York and New Brunswick makes a landing every trip."

ROBBINS' CORNERS—This was at the junction of Richmond and Rockland Avenues. The latter thoroughfare was sometimes called Petticoat Lane. The location took its name from Nathaniel Robbins, a dissolute character, who lived here during the Revolution.

SOUTH BEACH—What we now know as South Beach is that portion of the south shore where the first settlers located. Fifty years ago its hotels and fine bathing beach were well known attractions throughout the New York area.

ST. GEORGE—Location of the Staten Island General Post Office. It was probably named in honor of George Law, a prominent Grymes Hill resident and a well known engineer.

SKUNK'S MISERY—See Prince's Bay.

SPRINGVILLE—Sometimes called New Springville, this is the farming section of the Island. It occupies a portion of the Island known as Karle's Neck and was in 1836 called Karle's Neck Village.

SNUG HARBOR—Sailors' Snug Harbor, an institution for retired mariners, was established on the north shore of the Island about 1831, giving the locality its name.

STAPLETON—Named for William J. Staples in 1836, at which time it was known as New Ferry. It was sometimes called Second Landing. It is at the present time the principal east shore village and the location of Foreign Trade Zone No. 1.

TOMPKINSVILLE—Named in honor of Govenor Daniel D. Tompkins, who founded it about 1815. It is the site of the Watering Place, the spring which provided fresh water for shipping. During the eighteenth century a great part of it was a farm belonging to St. Andrew's Church known as the Glebe.

TOTTENVILLE—A village at the southernmost end of the Island, originally part of the Manor of Bentley, established in 1687 and probably occupied by Captain Christopher Billopp in 1675. Billopp's Ferry to Amboy dates from the seventeenth century. After the Revolution the region was called The Neck, and it was during this period that Tottens became numerous. Totten's Landing appears on the maps as well as Bentley Dock. The post office was Bentley until 1861 but has been Tottenville since 1862, except for a brief period in 1910 when it was Bentley Manor.

TRAVIS—Recently this village was known as Linoleumville and has at times been called Deckertown.

WEST NEW BRIGHTON—This locality, now one of the Island's most important towns, was originally part of Governor Dongan's Manor of Cassiltowne. Once a group of large farms, it developed rapidly after 1819, when Barrett's Dye Works were established. (See Factoryville.)

WILLOWBROOK—This locality was until recent years a spot of rural charm. It is now dominated by the huge Willowbrook State School.

WOODROW—A sparsely settled community lying between the Arthur Kill Road and Drumgoole Boulevard, noted for its beautiful Methodist Episcopal Church.

Stokes Mansion, New Brighton, built 1870. Demolished ca. **1930**. Photograph by Percy L. Sperr, **1928**. SIHS.

Fire Bell Tower, Stapleton. Postcard, ca. 1899.
SIHS.

Fire Bell Tower, Stapleton. Postcard, ca. 1899.
SIHS.

CHRONOLOGY

1524, April   : Giovanni da Verrazzano anchored in N. Y. Bay.

1609, Sept. 3: Henry Hudson anchored in the lower bay.

1630, Aug. 10: Patroon Michael Pauw received a grant, which included Staten Island, from the Dutch West India Co.

1636, Aug. 13: David deVries applied to Gov. van Twiller for possession of Staten Island, in order to plant a colony thereon.

1639,   : Colonists, arriving from Holland, sent to Staten Island by deVries.

1640, Jan. 7: Thomas Smythe leased plantation on Staten Island from deVries.

1640, July 16: Gov. Kieft sent punitive expedition from New Amsterdam to attack Indians on Staten Island.

1641, Sept. 1: deVries plantation destroyed by Indians in retaliation. (Pig War.)

1642, June 19: Greater portion of Staten Island granted to Cornelius Melyn.

1643,   : Indians attacked Island settlers. (Whiskey War.)

1644,   : Dutch organized an expedition against Staten Island Indians, who fled before the enemy's arrival.

1650, Dec. 19: Melyn and new colonists arrived at Staten Island from Holland.

1655, Sept. 16: Indians again destroyed settlement on Staten Island. (Peach War.)

1656, Jan. 26: Gov. Stuyvesant recommended abandonment of the Staten Island settlement because defence of the Island was difficult.

1660, Mar. 6: New treaty of peace with Indian chiefs.

1661, Aug.   : Stuyvesant considered application of nineteen Dutch and French, who presently settled upon Staten Island.

1663,   : Rev. Samuel Drisius began preaching on Staten Island.

1664, Aug. 18: English fleet anchored in Gravesend Bay and captured blockhouse on Staten Island.

1664, Aug. 29: New Amsterdam surrendered to English.

1670, Apr. 13: Gov. Francis Lovelace purchased Staten Island from the Indians. This was the final deed; earlier ones had been repudiated by the Indians.

1673, Aug. 8: A Dutch fleet recaptured New York.

1674, Nov. 10: With peace declared, English regained possession and Sir Edmund Andros became governor.

1676, Mar. 25: Patent was granted to Capt. Christopher Billopp, who seems to have been in possession of land at the southern end of Staten Island a year previous.

1679, Oct. 11, 12, 13: Jasper Dankers and Peter Sluyter, crossing the Narrows, came ashore and walked around Staten Island.

1680, Apr. 20: Gov. Andros declared all Indians free, and not subject to slavery.

1683,   : Rev. Petrus Tesschenmacker, Dutch minister, arrived at Staten Island. Gov. Thomas Dongan succeeded Andros.

1683, Nov. 1: Staten Island became Richmond County.

1687, Mar.   : There was filed a description of a survey of 340 acres in the eastern portion of the Island, later known as Duxbury Glebe.

1689,   : Leisler rebellion in New York.

1692,   : Gov. Benjamin Fletcher succeeded Dongan.

1693,   : Rev. David deBonrepos arrived to preach to French, English and Dutch.

1696,   : The Dutch received a lease of land in Cocclestown (Richmond) upon which stood the Voorlezer's house.

1698,   : Staten Island's population was 727, including slaves (10%).

1700,   : The Voorlezer's house sold.

1705,   : Rev. Aneas Mackenzie arrived upon Staten Island.

1711, Aug. 6: William Tillyer and wife gave deed for the site of St. Andrew's Church.

1718,   : Court was held at Stony Brook until about 1726.

1729,   : Court held for first time in first county courthouse, southeast corner of Richmond and Arthur Kill Roads.

1737,   : The Island's population was 1889, including 349 negro slaves.

1740,   : Ferry from Bay Ridge to Staten Island's east shore was established by Thomas Stillwell.

1747,   : Comes' Ferry from the north shore to New York established.

1755,   : Watson's Ferry from east shore to New York established.

1761, Oct.   : Gen. Jeffrey Amherst received Order of the Bath at a gala ceremony.

1763,   : Moravian Church at New Dorp consecrated.

1764,   : Sandy Hook lighthouse lighted for first time.

1771,   : Population 2847, including 594 negro slaves.

1771,   : Francis Asbury first preached here.

1775, May 22: First Provincial Congress met in New York; Staten Island was represented by five delegates.

1775, Dec. 6: Second Provincial Congress met, with Staten Island not represented. Upon being officially censured two delegates were elected.

1776, June 5: Congress ordered arrest of four Staten Islanders for conduct inimical to the cause of liberty.

1776, Apr. 15: British seamen at the Watering Place were fired upon by detachment of Americans under General Stirling.

1776, July 2-3: Nine thousand British troops landed on east shore.

1776, July 9: New York received news of the adoption of the Declaration of Independence.

1776, July 12: Twenty thousand British troops landed.

1776, Aug. 27: Battle of Long Island.

1776, Sept. 11: Conference in the Billopp House between Franklin, Rutledge, Adams and Lord Howe.

1776, Oct. 24: A detachment of American troops engaged the British in a skirmish near St. Andrew's Church.

1777, June 7: Capt. Andre composed his will at Richmondtown.

1777, July 23: Sir William Howe's army departed by transport.

1777, Aug. 22: Raid by fifteen hundred Americans under Gen. Sullivan.

1777, Oct. 7: Rev. Richard Charlton, rector of St. Andrew's, died in New York.

1778, June 5: Colonel Billopp captured.

1779, June 23: Colonel Billopp captured for the second time.

1780, Jan. 15: Gen. Stirling and twenty-five hundred troops crossed the Kill van Kull to attack the British on Staten Island.

1783, Nov. 25: British evacuated New York.

1783, Dec. 4: Last of British troops left Staten Island.

1785, : Baptist Church organized.

1787, : Woodrow Church was organized.

1788, Oct. : Rev. Richard Channing Moore became rector of St. Andrew's. (Incumbent until 1808.)

1799, : State of New York acquired thirty acres of the Duxbury Glebe for a quarantine.

1800, : Population 4564.

1801, : St. Andrew's rebuilt. Trinity Chapel erected.

1806, : Medical Society of Richmond County organized.

1807, : Daniel D. Tompkins elected governor of New York. (He became vice-president in 1817.)

1808, : Reformed Dutch Church in Richmondtown built.

1808, : Rev. David Moore succeeded his father as rector of St. Andrew's, beginning a forty-eight year rectorate.

1809, : Clove Meeting House was built.

1810, : Population 5347.

1812, : War of 1812; Staten Island forts manned by militia.

1814, : Gov. Tompkins came to live on Staten Island.

1814, : Fifty thousand dollars were appropriated to complete Fort Tompkins, until then but a series of earthworks.

1816, Mar. 31: Richmond Turnpike Company incorporated.

1820, : Population 6135.

1820, : Tompkinsville Reformed Dutch Church built upon land given by Vice-President Tompkins.

1824, Aug. 15: General Lafayette visited Daniel D. Tompkins at his home.

1825, June 1: Richmond Lodge, F. & A. Masons, recieved its charter.

1825, June 11: Death of Daniel D. Tompkins.

1825, July 4: Celebration in honor of the abolition of slavery on S. I.

1827, Oct. 17: "The Richmond Republican", first Staten Island newspaper, began publication. It was printed in New York.

1828, : Residence of Thomas E. Davis built. This later (1832) became the Pavilion Hotel.

1829, : County Poor House established.

1830, : Population 7082.

1831, : Sailors' Snug Harbor established on Staten Island; began operation 1833.

1832, Apr. 10: Rear Admiral Andrew E. K. Benham was born at New Dorp.

1833, Mar. 11: St. Paul's Episcopal Church organized.

1834, : Thomas E. Davis began development of New Brighton.

1836, July 19: Formal naming of the village of Stapleton.

1836, Sept. 14: Aaron Burr, one-time Vice-President of the U. S., died in Port Richmond.

1836, : Village of Richmond laid out by Henry I. Seaman.

1836, : Dr. Samuel MacKenzie Elliott, noted physician, acquired property at Bard Avenue and Richmond Terrace.

1837, : Seamen's Retreat, the old Marine Hospital, completed at Clifton.

1837, : Third County Courthouse in Richmondtown completed.

1837, July : "Richmond Co. Mirror", first newspaper printed on Island, starts publication.

1837, : Judge William Emerson came to live on Staten Island.

1838, : First bank established. (Closed 1842.)

1838, Mar. : A charter was granted the S. I. Whaling Co.

1839, Dec. 1: Mariners' Harbor M. E. Church was dedicated.

1839, : Robbin's Reef lighthouse in commission.

1840, : Population 10965.

1842, : The present Woodrow M. E. Church built.

1842, : Henry M. Boehm conducted a school at Green Ridge.

1842, Jan. 11: Tompkins Lyceum organized.

1843, : Henry David Thoreau lived for six months at Emerson Hill.

1843, Sept. 23: St. John's P. E. Church was organized.

1843, July 17: The parish of St. Luke's Church, Rossville, was formally organized.

1847,   : Capt. Jacob Vanderbilt purchased an estate at Grymes Hill.

1848,   : County Clerk's Office and Surrogate's Court, now the museum of the Staten Island Historical Society, was built.

1848, Oct. 1: The first service was held in the chapel of St. Mary's Episcopal Church.

1849, June 28: Christ Church organized.

1850,   : Population 15961.

1850,   : Sir Edward Cunard built "Bellevue" upon Grymes Hill.

1851,   : Giuseppi Garabaldi was on Staten Island 1851-53.

1851, Dec. 6: Reception to Louis Kossuth, Hungarian patriot.

1851,   : Garabaldi and Meucci opened a brewery in Rosebank which later became Bachmann's Brewery.

1851, Mar.   : The DeJonge Paper Factory began to operate on what is now known as Victory Boulevard.

1852, Oct. 17: German Evangelical Lutheran Church of St. John organized.

1853,   : Bechtel's Brewery founded.

1854,   : St. Simon's in the Clove began as a mission of St. John's, Clifton.

1854,   : Staten Island Clay Retort Works, established in New York by Balthasar Kreischer, was started at Kreischerville.

1856,   : George William Curtis came to Staten Island.

1856,   : Richmond County Gas Company organized.

1856,   : German Evangelical Lutheran Church of Stapleton organ'd.

1856, Jan. 23: Hagadorn's Staaten Islander, first newspaper to be printed on a power press on Staten Island, was published.

1856, Jan. 21: First meeting of the Staten Island Historical Society.

1858, Sept. 1-2: Quarantine buildings burned by S. I. citizens.

1860,   : Population 25492.

1860,   : Opening of the Staten Island Steam Railway.

1860,   : Magnetic telegraph to New York started operation.

1861,   : The "Dispensary", corner Bay and Union in Stapleton, was opened. During April of the same year it was named the S. R. Smith Infirmary. It is now S. I. Hospital.

1861,   : Tompkins Lyceum, later German Club Rooms, erected at Stapleton. (Van Duzer and Prospect Sts.)

1861,   : Staten Island Quartette Club organized.

1862, Mar. 17: The cornerstone of St. Patrick's R. C. Church, Richmondtown, laid.

1863,   : Horse car line chartered.

1863, Dec. 2: Local carpenters struck for two dollars per day.

1863, July   : Draft riots, originating in New York, spread to S. I.

1863, Nov. 20: The Ladies' Auxilliary of S. R. Smith Infirmary organ'd.

1864, June 20: S. R. Smith Infirmary located in old Quarantine grounds.

1865,   : The S. S. White Dental Works established.

1865, Oct. 24: Parish of the Church of the Holy Comforter organized.

1866, Mar. 22: Village of Edgewater incorporated.

1866, Apr. 24: Village of Port Richmond incorporated.

1866, Apr. 26: Village of New Brighton incorporated.

1866, Oct. 19: St. John's Guild organized.

1870,   : Population 33629.

1870,   : Rubsam and Horrmann Brewing Co. established.

1870,   : Police Department organized.

1871, July 30: Explosion of the ferryboat "Westfield".

1871,   : Edgewater Fire Dept. organized.

1872, Mar. 22: Staten Island Cricket Club founded.

1873, Aug. 31: Castleton Hill Moravian Church dedicated.

1874, Apr. 2: North Shore Fire Dept. organized.

1875, Sept. 8: Caleb Lyon, ex-governor of Idaho, died at Rossville.

1875, Dec. 28: Rev. Henry Boehm, associate of Bishop Asbury, died.

1876, Feb. 24: The first Charity Ball was held in the St. Mark's Hotel, New Brighton.

1876, June 15: Rev. Dr. Thomas S. Yocum became rector of St. Andrew's.

1877, Jan. 4: Commodore Cornelius Vanderbilt died, aged eighty-three.

1879,   : Staten Island Water Supply Co. incorporated.

1880,   : Population 38950.

1880,   : Lenhart Post No. 163, G. A. R. organized.

1881,   : Robert G. Shaw Post No. 112, G. A. R. organized.

1881, Nov. 12: The Natural Science Association organized.

1882,   : The Staten Island Diet Kitchen established at 18 Broad St.

1882, Nov. 2: Francis G. Shaw, author and philanthropist, died.

1883,   : The Crystal Water Works organized.

1883,   : St. Austin's School opened. (Now St. Vincent's Hospital.)

1884,   : Richmond Post No. 524, G. A. R. organized.

1884, Sept. 15: Staten Island Academy opened. (S. I. Day School.)

1885,   : Mount Loretto established.

1885,   : Rev. Canon Pascal Harrower began his rectorate of forty-three years.

1886, Feb. 23: Operation of ferry from St. George to New York began.

1886, Mar. 27: The "Richmond Co. Advance", a weekly newspaper, was established. It became a daily in 1918.

1886, June 25: Buffalo Bill's Wild West opened at Erastina.

1886, Aug : The Vanderbilt mausoleum was completed.

1887, June 21: Queen Victoria's Jubilee Celebration at Erastina at St. George.

1888, June 25: Sidney Howard Gay, abolitionist, died.

1888, July 4: Prohibition Park (Westerleigh) real estate development was begun.

1889, : Edgewater Village Hall was built. (Stapleton).

1889, : Hotel Castleton was built. (Burned 1907).

1890, : Population 51693.

1891, : The Westerleigh Collegiate Institute was opened.

1892, July 4: The first trolleys ran from Port Richmond to Meier's Corners.

1892, : George William Curtis died.

1894, : Tottenville re-incorporated.

1895, : The Staten Island Chamber of Commerce was organized.

1896, May 11: A bill creating the Greater New York became a law.

1896, : Tompkins department store was erected on Richmond Terrace.

1897, : The N. Y. & S. I. Electric Co. was incorporated.

1898, Jan. 1: George Cromwell, Republican, first president of the Borough of Richmond, took office.

1899, Feb. 6: The Tottenville Free Library was organized.

1900, : Population 67021.

1902, : The Actors' Home on Clove Road was founded.

1903, : St. Peter's R. C. Church, New Brighton, dedicated by Archbishop Farley.

1903, : St. Vincent's Hospital established.

1904, May 21: The cornerstone of the borough hall was laid.

1905, Sept. : The Richmond County Agricultural Society revived the county fairs at Dongan Hills for five years.

1906, May 2: The borough hall of St. George was dedicated.

1907, Nov. 12: The Hotel Castleton burned. (Built 1889).

1908, May 8: The Actors' Fund Home was opened.

1909, May : Richmond County Bar Association incorporated.

1913, Feb. 22: Dedication of site at Fort Wadsworth for American Indian.

1913, Nov. 12: Sea View Hospital was formally opened.

1917, Feb. 1: All existing post offices were consolidated with S. I. General P. O.

1917, June 30: William Winter, dramatic critic, died at New Brighton.

1917, Oct. 25: Staten Island began its use of Catskill water.

1917, : The S. R. Smith Infirmary became the Staten Island Hospital.

1918, : Wagner College moved from Rochester to Staten Island.

1920, : Population 116531.

1920, May 31: Hero Park was dedicated.

1921, Oct. 8: Trackless trolley line, Meier's Corners to Travis and to Seaview, was opened.

1922, Nov. 4: Official opening of the Richmond to Tottenville trackless trolley route.

1922, : Work was begun on a new Wagner College dormitory.

1923, July 31: Staten Island Edison Corp. purchased all existing electric business, property, and franchises.

1925, : Electrification of the steam railroad was accomplished.

1925, : Population 138227.

1927, Mar. 15: The Tysen Memorial Home for nurses (S. I. Hospital) was opened.

1928, June 14: The purchase of five hundred fifty-six acres (the Latourette site) approved by Board of Estimate.

1928, June 20: The Goethals Bridge and Outerbridge Crossing, both connecting Staten Island with New Jersey, were opened.

1929, Apr. 20: The Community Center on Victory Blvd. was dedicated.

1931, Nov. 14: The Bayonne-Staten Island Bridge opened from New Jersey to Staten Island.

1932, Apr. 8-16: A Home Exposition held in the Palma salesroom.

1932, May 28: The German Club Rooms burned.

1932, July : Faber Park swimming pool opened.

1932, Dec. : The new St. George Post Office opened.

1934, : The Russell Pavilion at the foot of Hylan Blvd. opened.

1935, Nov. 19: Construction of the Franklin D. Roosevelt boardwalk officially started.

1936, June 10: Staten Island Zoo opened.

1936, July 7: Joseph H. Lyons Playground opened.

1936, Sept. 14: **Tottenville and New Dorp High Schools opened.**

1936, Dec. 1: **Operation of Cromwell Center by Park Department begun.**

1940,   : The WPA completed a $144,000 project at Latourette Park.

1940, Mar. 7: Edwin Markham, 87, died.

1940,   : Population 174,441.

1945,   : Population 184,000. (N. Y. C. Board of Health estimate.)

1946,   : Population 187,000. (N. Y. C. Board of Health estimate.)

1946,   : The St. George Ferry Terminal was destroyed by fire.

1947,   : Population 190,000. (N. Y. C. Board of Health estimate.)

1948,   : Population 193,000. (N. Y. C. Board of Health estimate.)

1949,   : Federal authorities grant permission for erection of a bridge across the Narrows.

1949,   : Population 196,000. (N. Y. C. Board of Health estimate.)

INDEX

This revised edition was produced by the
Publishing Center for Cultural Resources.
The Publishing Center is a nonprofit organization founded in 1973 to help nonprofit
educational institutions and associations
become effective publishers. Its services,
which now extend to over 150 organizations
throughout the United States, are made possible by grants from public agencies and
private foundations and corporate contributions. The Publishing Center is located
in New York City.

History of SI

Leng & Davis